Shenandoah National Park Guidebook

Exploring Sky-High Peaks, Cascading Waterfalls, and Enchanting Wildlife Along the Scenic Skyline Drive

D1518240

Lovelyn Hill

Table of Contents

Introduction

Shenandoah National Park, a majestic expanse of natural beauty, stretches across the Blue Ridge Mountains in Virginia. This park, just 75 miles from the hustle and bustle of Washington, D.C., serves as a serene escape into nature's splendor. With over 200,000 acres of protected lands, Shenandoah is a haven for outdoor enthusiasts, offering breathtaking vistas, cascading waterfalls, and rich biodiversity.

The park's landscape is a mosaic of rolling hills, lush forests, and meandering streams, creating an enchanting environment for visitors. Skyline Drive, the park's main thoroughfare, winds its way along the crest of the mountains for 105 miles, providing countless opportunities to stop and admire the panoramic views. Each season paints the park in different hues, from the vibrant wildflowers of spring to the fiery foliage of autumn, ensuring a unique experience no matter when you visit.

Arriving at Shenandoah National Park, my adventure started with a scenic drive along Skyline Drive, the park's main artery. This 105-mile road winds along the crest of the Blue Ridge Mountains, offering stunning panoramic views at every turn. I made several stops at the park's 75 overlooks, each providing a unique perspective of the surrounding valleys and distant mountains.

One of my favorite stops was at the Dickey Ridge Visitor Center (milepost 4.6), where the grassy expanse and stone overlook offer sweeping views of the Shenandoah Valley. As I continued along Skyline Drive, I marveled at the changing scenery, from dense forests to open meadows, each more beautiful than the last.

Shenandoah is a hiker's paradise, with over 500 miles of trails ranging from easy walks to challenging climbs. I was particularly excited to explore some of the park's famous waterfalls. My first hike was to Dark Hollow Falls, a short but steep 1.4-mile round-trip that rewards hikers with a stunning 70-foot cascade. The trail, though challenging, was well worth the effort as the sound of rushing water and the cool mist from the falls provided a refreshing respite from the hike.

Another highlight was the hike to South River Falls, a longer and more strenuous 5.1-mile loop that leads to an 83-foot waterfall. This trail offers an observation deck and a chance to splash in the watering hole at the base of the falls, making it a perfect spot for a mid-hike break.

Shenandoah National Park is steeped in history, and I visited several historical sites during my stay. One particularly memorable experience was hiking to Rapidan Camp, the former summer retreat of President Herbert Hoover. This 2.1-mile hike (one way) through lush forests led to three restored cabins that offer a glimpse into the past. The site's tranquility and historical significance made it a standout part of my trip.

Another fascinating hike was along the Pocosin Trail, which features the ruins of the Upper Pocosin Mission. This trail provided a poignant reminder of the local mountain communities that once thrived in the area before the park was established.

One of the most thrilling aspects of my visit was encountering the park's diverse wildlife. Shenandoah is home to white-tailed deer, black bears, wild turkeys, and more than 200 bird species. Early mornings and late afternoons were the best times for wildlife spotting, and I was not disappointed. At Big Meadows, a prime wildlife viewing area, I saw numerous deer grazing and even spotted a black bear in the distance. The park's commitment to preserving its natural habitats ensures that these encounters are both frequent and respectful.

Shenandoah National Park is designated as a Dark Sky Park, making it an excellent destination for stargazing. One evening, I attended a night sky program at Big Meadows, where knowledgeable rangers provided telescopes and guided us through the constellations. Seeing the Milky Way stretch across the sky, unobstructed by light pollution, was a magical experience that I'll never forget. The clarity and brilliance of the stars were unlike anything I had seen before, and the experience deepened my appreciation for the park's natural beauty.

To fully immerse myself in the park's beauty, I chose to stay at the Big Meadows Lodge, which offers cozy rooms and cabins with stunning views. The lodge's rustic charm and modern amenities provided the perfect balance of comfort and nature. Each morning, I woke up to the sound of birdsong and the sight of the sun rising over the mountains, setting the tone for another day of exploration.

For those who prefer camping, Shenandoah offers numerous campgrounds that cater to all levels of campers. From the more developed Big Meadows Campground to the backcountry sites accessible only by foot, there's an option for everyone. The sense of community among campers and the opportunity to connect with nature made camping an appealing choice for many visitors I met along the trails.

No visit to Shenandoah would be complete without sampling the local cuisine. At Skyland's Pollock Dining Room, I enjoyed hearty meals with a view. The menu featured regional specialties like Virginia ham and apple cobbler, providing a delicious taste of the area's culinary traditions. For a more casual dining experience, the Wayside facilities along Skyline Drive offer grab-and-go options perfect for a quick lunch before hitting the trails again.

Therefore, my visit to Shenandoah National Park was more than just an adventure; it was a journey into nature's heart and a step back in time. From the breathtaking drives along Skyline Drive to the serene hikes through forested trails, every moment was filled with awe and wonder. The park's rich history, diverse wildlife, and stunning landscapes create a unique array of experiences that cater to all interests and ages.

Shenandoah's magic lies in its ability to offer something for everyone, whether you're seeking adventure, relaxation, or a deeper connection with nature. As I drove away from the park, I carried with me not just photographs and souvenirs, but a profound sense of peace and gratitude for having experienced one of America's true natural treasures.

If you ever find yourself yearning for a place where the mountains meet the sky, where waterfalls whisper ancient secrets, and where each star shines a little brighter, Shenandoah National Park awaits.

Geography of Shenandoah National Park

Shenandoah National Park, a sprawling expanse of natural beauty, is located in the heart of the Blue Ridge Mountains in Virginia. This park is a geographic marvel, stretching over 105 miles from north to south and encompassing more than 200,000 acres of protected land. It offers a diverse array of landscapes, from rolling hills and verdant forests to rugged peaks and tranquil streams.

Northern Terminus

The northern end of Shenandoah National Park begins near Front Royal, Virginia. This area is the gateway to the park for many visitors, featuring the Dickey Ridge Visitor Center, which provides essential information and resources for exploring the park. The park's northern boundary is marked by the Shenandoah River, a significant geographic feature that winds its way through the Shenandoah Valley. This region is characterized by gently rolling hills and lush woodlands, setting the stage for the park's scenic beauty.

Southern Terminus

At the southern end, the park extends to the area near Waynesboro, Virginia, and the Rockfish Gap entrance. This end of the park is equally captivating, featuring the Rockfish Valley Overlook, which provides sweeping views of the surrounding countryside. The southern terminus is also notable for its proximity to the Blue Ridge Parkway, another scenic drive that continues the natural splendor of Shenandoah beyond the park's boundaries.

The Stretch of the Blue Ridge Mountains

Shenandoah National Park is essentially a long, narrow strip of land running along the crest of the Blue Ridge Mountains. This range is part of the larger Appalachian Mountains and is known for its distinctive blue haze, caused by the release of volatile organic compounds from the trees. The park's highest peak is Hawksbill Mountain, which rises to 4,051 feet. This elevation provides panoramic views that are among the most breathtaking in the eastern United States.

Skyline Drive

Skyline Drive is the main thoroughfare that runs the length of Shenandoah National Park. This scenic roadway follows the ridge of the mountains, offering numerous overlooks and pull-offs where visitors can stop to admire the views. The drive is renowned for its beauty, particularly during the fall when the foliage transforms into a vibrant array of colors. Skyline Drive connects with the Blue Ridge Parkway at its southern end, creating a continuous route of scenic beauty that extends for hundreds of miles.

Major Peaks and Valleys

In addition to Hawksbill Mountain, Shenandoah National Park is home to several other notable peaks. Old Rag Mountain is perhaps the most famous, known for its challenging hike that involves rock scrambles and offers spectacular views from the summit. Other significant peaks include Stony Man Mountain and Mary's Rock, both of which provide stunning vistas and are popular with hikers.

The park's valleys are equally enchanting. The Shenandoah Valley lies to the west of the park and is a major geographical feature that has influenced the region's history and development. The valley is fertile and scenic, offering a contrast to the rugged terrain of the mountains. Within the park, you will find numerous smaller valleys and hollows, each with its unique charm. These include Whiteoak Canyon, known for its series of waterfalls, and Big Meadows, a large, open area that is a popular spot for wildlife viewing and stargazing.

Waterways and Waterfalls

Shenandoah National Park is crisscrossed by numerous streams and rivers, which contribute to the park's lush, green landscape. The park's waterways are integral to its ecosystem, providing habitats for a variety of plant and animal species. The Shenandoah River, which runs along the park's western boundary, is a key feature and a popular spot for fishing, kayaking, and canoeing.

Waterfalls are another highlight of the park's geography. Dark Hollow Falls, Rose River Falls, and South River Falls are just a few of the many cascades that attract visitors. These waterfalls are often the rewards of scenic hikes and are particularly beautiful in the spring when water levels are high from seasonal rains.

Ecological Zones

The park's varied elevation creates distinct ecological zones, each supporting different types of vegetation and wildlife. At lower elevations, you'll find dense hardwood forests dominated by oak, hickory, and tulip poplar. As you ascend, these forests give way to stands of chestnut oak and northern red oak. The highest elevations support unique plant communities, including mountain laurel and rhododendron thickets.

The diverse habitats within these ecological zones support a wide range of wildlife. Shenandoah is home to over 200 species of birds, 50 species of mammals, and numerous reptiles and amphibians. The park's wildlife includes black bears, white-tailed deer, bobcats, and various smaller mammals. Birdwatchers will find a paradise here, with opportunities to spot species such as the peregrine falcon, scarlet tanager, and pileated woodpecker.

Geology

The geology of Shenandoah National Park is as fascinating as its flora and fauna. The park's landscape has been shaped over millions of years by geological forces, resulting in a complex and diverse terrain. The Blue Ridge Mountains, where Shenandoah is located, are among the oldest mountains in the world, dating back over a billion years.

The park's bedrock is primarily composed of ancient granitic and metamorphic rocks. These rocks were formed deep within the Earth's crust and were later exposed by the erosion of overlying material. The distinctive greenstone found in the park is a type of metamorphosed basalt, which provides evidence of ancient volcanic activity. Quartzite and sandstone, remnants of ancient sea beds, can also be found, indicating that the area was once covered by shallow seas.

Human Impact and Conservation Efforts

The establishment of Shenandoah National Park involved significant human impact, particularly the displacement of families who lived on the land. In the 1920s and 1930s, the federal government acquired the land through eminent domain and private purchases, leading to the creation of the park. This history is preserved and interpreted at various sites within the park, offering visitors a glimpse into the lives of those who once called this area home.

Today, conservation efforts are a top priority for the National Park Service. The park is managed to preserve its natural and cultural resources while providing recreational opportunities for visitors. Initiatives such as the protection of endangered species, restoration of native plant communities, and efforts to mitigate the impacts of climate change are ongoing. The park also participates in the Leave No Trace program, promoting responsible outdoor ethics to minimize human impact on the environment.

Visitor Experience

Shenandoah National Park is designed to offer a comprehensive and enriching visitor experience. The park is equipped with several visitor centers, including the Dickey Ridge and Harry F. Byrd Sr. Visitor Centers. These centers provide educational exhibits, maps, and information to help visitors plan their trips. Rangers are available to answer questions and offer insights into the park's natural and cultural history.

Accommodations within the park range from campgrounds to rustic lodges, such as Big Meadows Lodge and Skyland Resort. These facilities provide comfortable lodging options and are well-situated for exploring the park's many attractions. For those who prefer a more primitive experience, backcountry camping is available, allowing visitors to immerse themselves in the park's wilderness.

Recreational opportunities abound in Shenandoah, from hiking and wildlife watching to fishing and horseback riding. The park's trails cater to all skill levels, offering everything from easy walks to challenging backcountry routes. The Appalachian Trail, which stretches over 2,000 miles from Georgia to Maine, passes through Shenandoah, providing an iconic hiking experience.

Climate and Weather Patterns of Shenandoah National Park

Shenandoah National Park offers a diverse and dynamic climate that changes with elevation and season. Understanding the park's weather patterns can help you plan your visit to maximize enjoyment and safety. This guide provides a detailed overview of Shenandoah's climate, including monthly temperatures, humidity levels, and the pros and cons of visiting during different times of the year.

Spring (March to May)

Spring in Shenandoah sees temperatures gradually rising from the cold of winter. March temperatures range from lows of around 30°F

(-1°C) to highs near 55°F (13°C). By May, temperatures climb to between 50°F (10°C) and 75°F (24°C). Humidity levels in spring are moderate, increasing as the season progresses.

Advantages for Tourism

- Wildflowers: Spring is the best time to see the park's famous wildflowers, which bloom in vibrant colors across the meadows and along trails.

- Milder Weather: The moderate temperatures are ideal for hiking and exploring without the extremes of summer heat or winter cold.

- Fewer Crowds: Early spring, particularly March, tends to be less crowded, providing a more serene experience.

Disadvantages for Tourism

- Variable Weather: Spring can be unpredictable, with sudden rain showers and lingering snow at higher elevations.

- Mud: Trails can be muddy due to melting snow and spring rains, making some paths slippery and difficult to navigate.

Summer (June to August)

Temperature and Humidity

Summer brings warm to hot temperatures, with highs ranging from 70°F (21°C) to 85°F (29°C) and occasional peaks above 90°F (32°C). Nighttime temperatures stay comfortably cool, usually between 50°F (10°C) and 65°F (18°C). Humidity levels are high, especially in July and August, contributing to a muggy atmosphere.

Advantages for Tourism

- Extended Daylight: Longer days provide more time for outdoor activities and exploration.

- Full Accessibility: All park facilities, trails, and roads are open and fully operational.

- Family-Friendly: Summer vacations make it a popular time for families to visit, with numerous ranger-led programs and activities.

Disadvantages for Tourism

- Heat and Humidity: High temperatures and humidity can make hiking strenuous and uncomfortable, particularly during midday.

- Crowds: Summer is the peak tourist season, leading to crowded trails, viewpoints, and accommodations.

- Thunderstorms: Afternoon thunderstorms are common, posing a risk for hikers and campers.

Autumn (September to November)

Fall in Shenandoah is marked by a dramatic drop in temperatures. September remains warm with highs around 75°F (24°C), but by November, temperatures can range from 30°F (-1°C) to 55°F (13°C). Humidity decreases significantly, making the air crisp and dry.

Advantages for Tourism

- Fall Foliage: Autumn is arguably the most beautiful season, with spectacular fall colors peaking in mid to late October.

- Comfortable Hiking: Cooler temperatures and lower humidity create perfect conditions for hiking and outdoor activities.

- Wildlife Viewing: Animals are more active as they prepare for winter, offering excellent opportunities for wildlife photography.

Disadvantages for Tourism

- Variable Weather: Rapid temperature changes can occur, and early snowfalls at higher elevations are possible in late autumn.

- Crowds: The fall foliage season attracts many visitors, especially on weekends, leading to crowded conditions similar to summer.

Winter (December to February)

Winter is cold, with temperatures often dropping below freezing. December sees highs around 45°F (7°C) and lows near 25°F (-4°C), while January and February can be even colder, with lows dipping to 20°F (-6°C) or lower. Humidity is relatively low, but winter storms can bring heavy snowfall.

Advantages for Tourism

- Solitude: Winter offers the most solitude, as few tourists brave the cold. You can enjoy peaceful, quiet landscapes.

- Snow Scenery: Snow-covered vistas and frozen waterfalls create a magical winter wonderland.

- Winter Sports: Opportunities for snowshoeing and cross-country skiing are available, providing a different way to experience the park.

Disadvantages for Tourism

- Cold Temperatures: The frigid weather can be challenging for prolonged outdoor activities.

- Limited Accessibility: Some park facilities and roads, including portions of Skyline Drive, may close due to snow and ice.

- Shorter Days: Limited daylight hours restrict the time available for outdoor exploration.

Monthly Climate Breakdown

- March: Transition month with variable conditions; temperatures range from 30°F to 55°F; moderate humidity.

- April: Warmer, with highs of 45°F to 65°F; wildflowers start to bloom.

- May: Mild and pleasant, with temperatures from 50°F to 75°F; ideal for hiking.

- June: Start of summer; temperatures between 60°F and 80°F; increasing humidity.

- July: Hottest month; highs can reach 90°F; high humidity and frequent thunderstorms.

- August: Similar to July; slightly cooler towards the end; continued high humidity.

- September: Cooling down; temperatures from 55°F to 75°F; lower humidity.

- October: Peak foliage month; temperatures from 40°F to 65°F; crisp and dry air.

- November: Cooling significantly; temperatures between 30°F and 55°F; early snow possible.

- December: Winter begins; highs around 45°F; potential for snow.

- January: Coldest month; lows around 20°F; snow and ice common.

- February: Similar to January; temperatures gradually begin to rise towards the month's end.

Tourism Considerations

Advantages of Spring and Fall

- Moderate temperatures and humidity.

- Spectacular natural displays (wildflowers in spring, foliage in fall).

- Generally fewer crowds compared to summer.

Disadvantages of Summer

- High temperatures and humidity can make outdoor activities very uncomfortable.

- Crowded conditions at popular sites and trails.

- Increased risk of thunderstorms.

Advantages of Winter

- Solitude and peaceful landscapes.

- Unique winter scenery and activities.

- Lower accommodation rates and fewer visitors.

Disadvantages of Winter

- Cold temperatures and shorter days limit outdoor activities.

- Possible road and trail closures due to snow and ice.

- Higher risk of hypothermia and frostbite for unprepared visitors.

Rich History of Shenandoah National Park

Early Beginnings: Before the Park

The history of Shenandoah National Park is deeply rooted in the lives of the Native American tribes and early European settlers who inhabited the Blue Ridge Mountains. The Monacan and Manahoac tribes used these mountains for seasonal migrations, hunting, and gathering. By the 18th century, European settlers began establishing homesteads, farming, and building communities within the lush valleys and forested slopes.

The Formation of the Park: Displacement and Development

In 1926, Congress authorized the creation of Shenandoah National Park, leading to significant changes in the lives of the local residents. Over 400 families were displaced to make way for the park. This process involved a combination of land purchases, donations, and, controversially, the use of eminent domain. The displaced families left behind a rich cultural legacy that includes family cemeteries, old homesteads, and artifacts, some of which can still be found within the park boundaries today.

The Role of the Civilian Conservation Corps (CCC)

The establishment and development of Shenandoah National Park were significantly influenced by the efforts of the Civilian Conservation Corps (CCC). As part of President Franklin D. Roosevelt's New Deal, the CCC was created in 1933 to provide jobs and aid in the nation's recovery from the Great Depression. Young, unemployed men were recruited to work on various conservation projects, and Shenandoah National Park became one of their prominent sites.

Infrastructure Development

Between 1933 and 1942, approximately 10,000 young men from the CCC lived and worked in Shenandoah. They played a crucial role in developing the park's infrastructure, which included the construction of Skyline Drive, a scenic 105-mile road that runs along the crest of the Blue Ridge Mountains. This iconic drive offers visitors stunning vistas and easy access to many of the park's attractions.

The CCC's accomplishments in Shenandoah were vast. They built trails, fire roads, and overlooks; planted thousands of trees and shrubs; and constructed facilities such as campgrounds and picnic areas. Their work not only provided immediate relief and employment during the Great Depression but also laid the foundation for the park's long-term sustainability and accessibility.

Daily Life and Legacy

Life in the CCC camps was regimented and structured. The young men, typically aged 18 to 25, worked six days a week on various conservation projects. They received training, uniforms, shelter, and three meals a day. Despite the hard labor, many CCC workers appreciated the opportunity to learn new skills, earn money, and contribute to a greater cause. The $30 monthly wage, of which $25 was sent home to their families, provided much-needed financial support during difficult economic times.

The legacy of the CCC extends beyond the physical infrastructure they built. Many of these men later served in World War II, and the skills and discipline they developed in the CCC camps proved invaluable. The annual CCC reunions held at Shenandoah National Park celebrate their contributions and keep their stories alive for future generations.

Cultural Heritage and Preservation

The displaced residents left behind numerous cultural artifacts, including tools, household items, and remnants of their homes. These artifacts provide a glimpse into the daily lives of the mountain families and are preserved in park museums and interpretive centers. Family cemeteries, which were often left undisturbed, are scattered throughout the park, serving as solemn reminders of the people who once called these mountains home.

Continuing Preservation and Education

Today, Shenandoah National Park is not only a place of natural beauty but also a living museum of American history. The park offers numerous educational programs and exhibits that explore its rich cultural and natural heritage. Visitors can learn about the history of the CCC at the Byrd Visitor Center and participate in ranger-led programs that highlight the stories of displaced families and the early settlers of the region.

The park's preservation efforts continue, with ongoing projects to maintain and restore its historic structures and landscapes. Through these efforts, Shenandoah National Park remains a vibrant example of the balance between conservation and recreation, offering visitors a chance to connect with both nature and history.

Shenandoah National Park's history is a complex tapestry of natural beauty, human resilience, and dedicated conservation efforts. From the early Native American inhabitants to the European settlers, the displaced families, and the hardworking men of the CCC, each era has left its mark on the park, creating a legacy that continues to inspire and educate visitors today

Practical Advice and Travel Tips for Tourists

Best Time to Visit

Shenandoah National Park is a year-round destination, but timing your visit can significantly impact your experience. The best time to visit is in late spring (April to May) and early fall (September to October). During these periods, the weather is mild, and the park's natural beauty is at its peak with blooming wildflowers in the spring and vibrant fall foliage.

Entrance Fees and Passes

Entrance to Shenandoah National Park requires a fee. A 7-day passenger vehicle pass costs $30, while a motorcycle pass is $25. If you plan to visit multiple national parks, consider purchasing the America the Beautiful Pass for $80, which grants access to over 2,000 federal recreation sites across the country.

Navigating the Park

Skyline Drive

Skyline Drive is the park's main thoroughfare, stretching 105 miles from Front Royal to Waynesboro. It offers breathtaking views and access to numerous trailheads and overlooks. The speed limit is 35 mph, allowing you to safely enjoy the scenery. Note that the drive can be congested during peak seasons, so starting your journey early in the morning is advisable.

Visitor Centers

The park has two main visitor centers: The Dickey Ridge Visitor Center near Front Royal and the Harry F. Byrd Visitor Center at Big Meadows. Both centers provide maps, exhibits, and helpful information about park activities. Rangers are available to answer questions and provide recommendations tailored to your interests.

Hiking Tips

Shenandoah features over 500 miles of trails, catering to all skill levels from easy walks to challenging hikes. Highlights include Old Rag Mountain and Dark Hollow Falls. To enhance your hiking experience, consider these tips:

- Start Early: To avoid crowds and the midday heat, begin your hikes early in the morning.

- Stay on the Trails: This helps protect the environment and reduces the risk of injury.

- Bring Essentials: Pack plenty of water, snacks, a map, and a first aid kit. Wear appropriate footwear and clothing layers to adapt to changing weather conditions.

- Wildlife Awareness: Keep a safe distance from wildlife and carry bear spray as a precaution.

Camping and Lodging

Campgrounds

Shenandoah offers several campgrounds, including Big Meadows, Lewis Mountain, and Loft Mountain. These campgrounds provide basic amenities and are well-situated for exploring different areas of the park. Reservations are recommended, especially during peak seasons. If you prefer backcountry camping, obtain a free permit and familiarize yourself with the park's regulations.

Lodging

For a more comfortable stay, consider lodging options such as Skyland Resort or Big Meadows Lodge. These historic lodges offer modern amenities and stunning views of the park. Booking in advance is crucial during the busy months.

Safety Tips

Weather Preparedness

The weather in Shenandoah can be unpredictable, especially at higher elevations. Check the forecast before your trip and pack accordingly. Layers are essential, as temperatures can vary significantly throughout the day.

Wildlife Encounters

While wildlife sightings are a highlight of visiting Shenandoah, it's important to stay safe. Black bears are common, so make noise while hiking to avoid surprising them. Store food securely and never feed wildlife. If you encounter a bear, back away slowly and do not run.

Trail Safety

Many injuries in the park are caused by slips and falls on wet rocks, especially near waterfalls. Enjoy these natural features from a safe distance and stick to designated viewpoints. Always inform someone of your plans and expected return time if hiking alone.

Activities and Attractions

Waterfalls and Scenic Overlooks

Shenandoah is renowned for its stunning waterfalls and scenic overlooks. Dark Hollow Falls is one of the park's most accessible waterfalls, while Hawksbill Mountain offers one of the best panoramic views. Make sure to bring your camera to capture these picturesque spots.

Ranger Programs and Special Events

Participate in ranger-led programs to learn more about the park's natural and cultural history. Special events, such as the Night Sky Festival, offer unique experiences like stargazing and educational talks. Check the park's calendar for upcoming events during your visit.

River Activities

Consider floating down the South Fork of the Shenandoah River. This relaxing activity provides a different perspective of the park and its surrounding landscapes. Depending on river conditions, you can choose between kayaking, canoeing, or rafting. Local outfitters offer guided trips and equipment rentals.

Dining and Supplies

While the park has some dining options at its lodges and visitor centers, you may want to explore nearby towns like Luray and Front Royal for more variety. These towns offer a of restaurants, from casual eateries to fine dining. Stock up on supplies before entering the park, as options within the park are limited and can be more expensive.

Therefore, in this guidebook, you will find comprehensive information to help plan your visit, including practical advice, historical insights, and tips for making the most of your time in Shenandoah National Park. Whether you're a seasoned hiker or a first-time visitor, this guide will provide all the details you need for an unforgettable experience.

In the next chapter, we will discuss essential aspects of planning your visit to Shenandoah National Park. Each section will provide detailed information to help you prepare for your adventure.

Chapter 1: Planning Your Trip

Best Time to Visit Shenandoah National Park

Shenandoah National Park offers unique experiences throughout the year, each season bringing its own set of highlights.

Spring (March to May)

This is reasonably the best time to visit. The park bursts into life with blooming wildflowers and vibrant greenery. Temperatures range from 35°F in March to 55°F in May, making it ideal for hiking and exploring. Spring also sees the return of many migratory bird species, making it a prime time for birdwatching. Facilities and services begin to reopen after the winter, and you can enjoy the fresh, rejuvenated landscape with fewer crowds than in the peak summer months.

Summer (June to August)

Summer brings warmer temperatures, averaging around 65°F but sometimes reaching the mid-80s. This is the busiest time of the year due to school vacations. Despite the crowds, summer is perfect for enjoying long days of hiking, picnicking, and exploring the park's numerous waterfalls to their fullest. However, it's wise to start activities early in the day to avoid midday heat and larger crowds.

Fall (September to November)

Fall is spectacular in Shenandoah National Park, with the foliage transforming into brilliant shades of red, orange, and yellow. The peak foliage typically occurs in mid-October, drawing visitors from all over to experience the breathtaking views along Skyline Drive. Fall temperatures are cooler, making for comfortable hiking conditions. This season also offers clear skies for stargazing and a variety of wildlife sightings as animals prepare for winter.

Winter (December to February)

Winter is the quietest season in Shenandoah. While many facilities close and temperatures drop significantly, the park takes on a serene, snowy beauty. This is a great time for those seeking solitude and enjoying activities like winter hiking, birdwatching, and even ice climbing in areas like Whiteoak Canyon and Overall Run Falls. Be prepared for cold weather and potentially icy conditions on the roads and trails.

Crowd Levels

Peak Season (June to October): Shenandoah sees the highest number of visitors during the summer and early fall, especially from late June through October. Weekends and holidays during this period can be particularly crowded. To avoid the throngs, try visiting on weekdays and starting your day early. Parking lots at popular trailheads like Old Rag Mountain and Dark Hollow Falls fill up quickly, so arriving early ensures you get a spot and can enjoy the trails in relative peace.

Shoulder Seasons (April to May, November): The spring and late fall months are excellent for avoiding peak crowds while still enjoying mild weather. April and May offer blooming wildflowers and fewer visitors, making it a great time for hiking and wildlife watching. November, just after the peak fall foliage, provides cooler temperatures and a more tranquil environment as the number of visitors decreases significantly.

Off-Season (December to March): Winter is the least crowded time in Shenandoah. The cold weather and occasional snow deter many visitors, but those who brave the elements are rewarded with serene landscapes and quiet trails. This is also the best time for stargazing, as the crisp, clear winter skies offer unparalleled views of the night sky. Ensure you check weather conditions and road closures before setting out.

Special Events

Shenandoah National Park hosts several annual events and festivals that highlight its natural beauty and cultural heritage.

Wildflower Weekend (May): This event celebrates the park's diverse flora, with guided walks, talks, and activities centered around the blooming wildflowers. It's a fantastic opportunity to learn about the park's ecosystem and enjoy the vibrant spring scenery.

Night Sky Festival (August): Held in late summer, this festival focuses on stargazing and astronomy. Participants can enjoy ranger-led programs, telescope viewings, and talks by guest astronomers. It's an excellent time to explore the park after dark and experience the beauty of the night sky.

Fall Foliage Festival (October): October brings the peak of fall colors, and the park celebrates with various activities, including guided hikes and scenic drives. The festival draws visitors to witness the spectacular autumn hues that blanket the park's landscapes.

Junior Ranger Day (April): This family-friendly event offers a range of educational activities for children, helping them learn about the park's natural and cultural history while earning their Junior Ranger badges.

Wildlife Viewing Events: Throughout the year, the park organizes events focused on wildlife observation, such as birdwatching tours in the spring and black bear tracking in the fall. These events provide insights into the behaviors and habitats of the park's diverse wildlife.

How to Get to Shenandoah National Park

Nearest Airports

When planning your trip to Shenandoah National Park, selecting the nearest airport is crucial for a smooth journey. Here are the major airports closest to the park:

Charlottesville-Albemarle Airport (CHO)

Located in Charlottesville, Virginia, this airport is approximately 25.5 miles from the park, making it the closest airport to Shenandoah. CHO offers several daily flights to major cities like New York-LaGuardia, Charlotte, and Washington-Dulles. Car rental services are available from companies such as AVIS, National Car Rental, Budget, and Enterprise, which you can find at the airport's car rental center. From the airport, you can drive to the park's Swift Run Gap Entrance in about 30 minutes, the closest entry point.

Washington Dulles International Airport (IAD)

Located in Washington, D.C., about 65.4 miles from Shenandoah, Washington Dulles is a major international airport offering numerous domestic and international flights. It is a convenient option for travelers from various parts of the world. From IAD, you can drive to the Front Royal Entrance in approximately 1 hour and 5 minutes. The airport also provides extensive transportation options, including bus services, taxi services, and car rentals from companies like Enterprise, National, Alamo, Hertz, and more.

Roanoke-Blacksburg Regional Airport (ROA)

Situated in Roanoke, Virginia, this airport is around 79 miles from Shenandoah. ROA serves as a gateway for travelers coming from various parts of the country. It offers car rental services and taxi options to get you to the park. The drive from ROA to the park takes about 1 hour and 45 minutes.

Shenandoah Valley Regional Airport (SHD)

Located in Weyers Cave, Virginia, SHD is approximately 55.5 miles from Shenandoah National Park. It offers a range of flights and is particularly convenient for those traveling from nearby states. Rental car services are available at the airport, facilitating an easy drive to the park. The travel time from SHD to the park is roughly 1 hour.

Richmond International Airport (RIC)

Located in Richmond, Virginia, about 107.5 miles from Shenandoah, RIC is a major airport in the region. It offers numerous flight options and rental car services, making it a viable choice for visitors planning to explore other parts of Virginia as well. The drive from RIC to Shenandoah takes around 2 hours.

Driving Directions

Driving to Shenandoah National Park from various major cities offers a scenic and convenient way to begin your adventure. Here are detailed directions from several key locations:

Washington, D.C.

From Washington, D.C., head west on I-66 towards Front Royal. Exit onto Route 340 South, which leads you directly to the park's Front Royal Entrance. This route is about 70 miles and takes approximately 1 hour and 30 minutes. Alternatively, you can access Thornton Gap by continuing on I-66 and taking US-211 West towards Luray.

Richmond, VA

From Richmond, take I-64 West to Charlottesville. Then, head north on US-29 to US-33 West, leading you to the Swift Run Gap Entrance. This drive covers about 100 miles and takes around 2 hours. Another option is to continue on I-64 West past Charlottesville and take US-250 West to the Rockfish Gap Entrance, about 107.5 miles from Richmond.

Baltimore, MD

From Baltimore, drive west on I-70 and merge onto US-340 South towards Charles Town, WV. Follow US-340 South to Front Royal and enter the park through the Front Royal Entrance. The journey is approximately 100 miles and takes around 2 hours and 30 minutes.

Philadelphia, PA

From Philadelphia, take I-76 West (Pennsylvania Turnpike) to Harrisburg. Then, follow I-81 South to Front Royal, where you can enter the park through the Front Royal Entrance. This drive is about 190 miles and takes approximately 4 hours.

Charlotte, NC

From Charlotte, head north on I-77 to I-81 North. Continue on I-81 North to New Market, then take US-211 East to the Thornton Gap Entrance. This route covers approximately 300 miles and takes around 5 hours and 30 minutes.

Public Transportation

While driving is the most common way to reach Shenandoah National Park, there are public transportation options available for those who prefer not to drive.

Virginia Breeze

Virginia Breeze operates a bus service from Washington Dulles International Airport to various locations in the Shenandoah Valley, including stops near the park. This service is convenient for travelers arriving by air who prefer not to rent a car. From the bus stop, you can take a taxi or a shuttle service to the park's entrance.

Amtrak

Amtrak provides train service to several stations near Shenandoah National Park. The closest station is in Charlottesville, which is serviced by the Cardinal, Crescent, and Northeast Regional lines. From the Charlottesville station, you can rent a car or take a taxi to reach the park, which is about 30 miles away.

Local Transit

Once you are in the region, local transit options like taxis and ride-sharing services (Uber and Lyft) are available to take you to the park.

Some local shuttle services also operate in the area, providing transportation from nearby towns and cities to Shenandoah's entrances.

Park Shuttles

During peak seasons, Shenandoah National Park occasionally offers shuttle services that run between key locations within the park. These shuttles can help you navigate between popular trailheads and visitor centers without the need for a personal vehicle. Check the park's official website for current shuttle schedules and availability.

Entrance Fees and Passes

Fee Structure

Shenandoah National Park charges various entrance fees depending on the type of visit. Understanding the fee structure can help you plan your budget effectively.

Single-Day and Multi-Day Passes

- Private Vehicle: $30 for a 7-day pass, covering unlimited entries for the vehicle and its passengers for seven consecutive days.

- Motorcycle: $25 for a 7-day pass, covering the motorcycle and its rider.

- Per Person: $15 for individuals entering on foot, bicycle, or horseback, valid for seven consecutive days.

- Commercial Vehicles: Fees vary based on the vehicle's capacity. For example, a commercial van (7-15 seats) costs $75, while a motor coach (26+ seats) is $200.

- Non-Commercial Group: $15 per person for groups of 16 or more, with no charge for those under 16.

Annual Passes

- Shenandoah Annual Pass: $55, providing unlimited entry for one year to the pass holder and passengers in the same vehicle (up to four adults, with no charge for children under 16).

America the Beautiful Passes

- Annual Pass: $80, providing access to over 2,000 federal recreation sites, including all national parks.

- Annual Senior Pass: $20 for U.S. citizens and permanent residents aged 62 and above.

- Lifetime Senior Pass: $80 for U.S. citizens and permanent residents aged 62 and above.

- Annual Military Pass: Free for current U.S. military members and their dependents.

- Lifetime Military Pass: Free for Gold Star Families and U.S. military veterans.

- Access Pass: Free for U.S. citizens or permanent residents with disabilities.

- Fourth Grade Pass: Free for U.S. fourth graders and their families.

Purchase Options

Purchasing passes in advance can save you time and ensure a smoother entry into Shenandoah National Park.

Online Purchase

Passes can be bought online through the National Park Service website at www.nps.gov/shen/planyourvisit/fees.htm or Recreation.gov. This option is convenient and allows you to avoid long lines at the park entrances.

In-Person Purchase

Passes are available at all park entrance stations, including:

- Front Royal Entrance (mile 0)

- Thornton Gap Entrance (mile 31.5)

- Swift Run Gap Entrance (mile 65.5)

- Rockfish Gap Entrance (mile 104.6)

You can pay by cash or credit/debit card at most entrances, ensuring flexibility for all visitors.

Advantages of Purchasing Passes in Advance

- Avoiding Delays: Buying your pass online helps you bypass the ticket lines at entrance stations, especially during peak seasons.

- Guaranteed Access: During busy periods, having a pre-purchased pass ensures you won't be turned away due to capacity limits.

- Special Passes: Some passes, such as the Old Rag Mountain day-use ticket, must be reserved in advance due to high demand. These tickets can be purchased online up to 30 days before your visit and are essential for accessing certain popular areas.

Discounts and Free Entry Days

Shenandoah National Park offers various discounts and designated free entry days to make visiting more accessible.

Discounts

- Senior Citizens: U.S. citizens and permanent residents aged 62 or older can purchase discounted annual ($20) or lifetime ($80) passes.

- Military Personnel: Active-duty military members and their dependents can obtain a free annual pass, while veterans and Gold Star Families are eligible for a free lifetime pass.

- Students: Fourth graders can receive a free annual pass through the Every Kid Outdoors program, which grants access to the pass holder and accompanying family members.

Free Entry Days

Shenandoah National Park waives entrance fees on specific days throughout the year, including:

- Martin Luther King, Jr. Day (January 15)

- First Day of National Park Week (April 20)

- Juneteenth National Independence Day (June 19)

- Anniversary of the Great American Outdoors Act (August 4)

- National Public Lands Day (September 28)

- Veterans Day (November 11)

These fee-free days are an excellent opportunity to explore the park without the cost of an entrance fee. However, it's important to note that other fees, such as for camping or special tours, are still applicable.

Visitor Centers and Facilities

Main Visitor Centers

Dickey Ridge Visitor Center

Located at Mile 4.6 on Skyline Drive, Dickey Ridge Visitor Center is the first stop for many visitors entering Shenandoah National Park from the north, near Front Royal, Virginia. The center is open from mid-April through November, with operating hours from 9:00 a.m. to

5:00 p.m. Sunday through Thursday, and until 6:00 p.m. on Fridays and Saturdays.

Dickey Ridge offers a range of services to help you get oriented with the park. The information desk provides maps, brochures, and helpful tips from knowledgeable rangers. Interactive exhibits and a short film offer insights into the park's natural and cultural history. The center also includes a bookstore where you can purchase guides, souvenirs, and educational materials. Restrooms and picnic areas are available nearby, making it a convenient stop before you head deeper into the park.

Harry F. Byrd Visitor Center

Located at Mile 51 on Skyline Drive, Harry F. Byrd Visitor Center is situated in the heart of Shenandoah National Park, near Big Meadows. This center is open year-round, with operating hours from 9:00 a.m. to 5:00 p.m. Sunday through Thursday, and until 6:00 p.m. on Fridays and Saturdays.

The Harry F. Byrd Visitor Center features extensive exhibits detailing the park's history, geology, and wildlife. A highlight is the interactive displays that engage visitors of all ages. The center also shows a 12-minute film about the park, offering an excellent introduction to what you can expect during your visit. The information desk here is staffed with rangers who can provide advice, maps, and information on ranger-led programs. Like Dickey Ridge, this center also has a bookstore and restrooms.

Facilities and Amenities

Campgrounds

Shenandoah National Park offers several campgrounds to accommodate visitors:

- Mathews Arm Campground: Located at Mile 22.2, this campground is currently undergoing electrical repairs but typically operates from spring to late October.

- Big Meadows Campground: Situated at Mile 51.2, this campground is open from late March to early December and requires reservations.

- Lewis Mountain Campground: Found at Mile 57.5, this campground operates on a first-come, first-served basis from late March to early December.

- Loft Mountain Campground: Located at Mile 79.5, it is open from May to late October and offers both reservation and first-come, first-served sites.

Picnic Areas

The park features several picnic areas, each equipped with tables and grills:

- Dickey Ridge (Mile 4.7)

- Elkwallow (Mile 24.1)

- Pinnacles (Mile 36.7)

- Big Meadows (Mile 51.2)

- Lewis Mountain (Mile 57.5)

- South River (Mile 62.8)

- Dundo (Mile 83.7)

These areas are open year-round, though water and fire availability may be limited.

Dining Options

Dining options within the park include

- Skyland Resort (Miles 41.7 and 42.5): Offers dining, a tap room, and grab-and-go food.

- Big Meadows Lodge (Mile 51.2): Provides dining, a tap room, and grab-and-go food.

- Waysides: Located at Elkwallow (Mile 24), Big Meadows (Mile 51.2), and Loft Mountain (Mile 79.5), these offer snacks, gifts, and camping supplies.

Accessibility

Shenandoah National Park strives to be accessible to all visitors, including those with disabilities. Both main visitor centers are equipped with ramps and accessible restrooms. Additionally, exhibits and film presentations are designed to be accessible, with features such as captioning and assistive listening devices.

Trails and Facilities

Some trails and facilities in the park are designed to accommodate wheelchairs and visitors with mobility challenges. The Limberlost Trail, for example, is a fully accessible trail offering a peaceful walk through the forest with occasional benches along the path.

Special Services

Rangers at both visitor centers can provide information on accessible services and facilities. Service animals are welcome throughout the park, and there are designated parking spaces at most major attractions and facilities. If you have specific accessibility needs, contacting the park in advance can ensure a smoother visit.

In conclusion, Chapter 1 provides essential information for preparing your visit to Shenandoah National Park. It covers the best times to visit, emphasizing late spring and early fall for optimal weather and fewer crowds. Detailed directions from major cities and nearby airports, such as Washington Dulles International and Charlottesville-Albemarle, are provided to help you reach the park easily. Information on entrance fees, available passes, and visitor centers like Dickey Ridge and Byrd Visitor Center is included to ensure a well-informed trip.

In the next chapter, however, we will explore various accommodation options within and near Shenandoah National Park. This chapter will detail campgrounds, lodges, and nearby hotels, offering a range of choices to suit different preferences and budgets. Stay tuned for in-depth details on each accommodation option to make the most of your visit to Shenandoah National Park.

Chapter 2: Accommodation Options

In this chapter, we'll explore various accommodation options to ensure a comfortable and enjoyable stay in Shenandoah National Park. From rustic campgrounds to cozy lodges, each section will provide detailed information on amenities, pricing, and unique features to help you choose the perfect lodging for your adventure.

Campgrounds Within the Park

Big Meadows Campground

Big Meadows Campground is centrally located within Shenandoah National Park at Mile 51.2 on Skyline Drive. This makes it an ideal base for exploring the park's many attractions, including Dark Hollow Falls and Byrd Visitor Center. The campground is surrounded by picturesque meadows and offers easy access to several hiking trails, providing campers with beautiful scenic views and abundant wildlife.

Location/Address

Big Meadows Campground, Skyline Drive Mile 51.2, Shenandoah National Park, Virginia

Amenities

- Campsites: The campground features 221 sites suitable for tents, trailers, and RVs, with some sites offering generator-free loops for a quieter experience.

- Facilities: Amenities include restrooms, showers (available for a fee), picnic tables, fire rings with grills, and a camp store. There is also a dump station and potable water available.

- Additional Features: The campground offers easy access to trails, ranger-led programs, and a nearby lodge with dining options.

Contact Information

- Phone Number: 540-999-3500

- Emergency Phone: 1-800-732-0911

Price Range

The nightly rate for campsites is approximately $30. Showers are available for an additional fee ($5 for 10 minutes). Prices are subject to change.

Unique Features and Scenic Views

Big Meadows Campground is renowned for its stunning meadows, which are particularly beautiful during the spring wildflower bloom and the vibrant fall foliage. The campground's central location provides convenient access to some of the park's most popular trails, including the Appalachian Trail and Dark Hollow Falls Trail.

Loft Mountain Campground

Loft Mountain Campground, perched atop Big Flat Mountain, is one of the largest and most popular campgrounds in Shenandoah National Park. This campground offers a wilderness experience with the convenience of modern amenities, making it a favored spot for both novice and seasoned campers. It is also a pet-friendly campground.

Location/Address

Loft Mountain Campground is located at mile 79.5 on Skyline Drive. The physical address is 3655 U.S. Highway 211 East, Luray, VA 22835. This prime location provides stunning views of the surrounding Blue Ridge Mountains and easy access to numerous trails and scenic overlooks.

Amenities

The campground is well-equipped with various amenities to enhance your camping experience:

- Campsites: 205 sites for tents, trailers, and RVs (up to 30 feet)

- Restrooms: Flush toilets

- Showers: Coin-operated hot showers

- Laundry: Coin-operated laundry facilities

- Camp Store: Supplies, firewood, and other essentials

- Picnic Tables and Fire Rings: Each site comes with a picnic table and fire ring

- Bear Boxes: Food storage to prevent wildlife encounters

- Dump Station: Available for RVs

- Recycling and Trash Disposal: Convenient locations throughout the campground.

Contact Information

For more information or specific inquiries:

- Phone: 540-999-3500

- Emergency Phone: 1-800-732-0911

Price Range

The cost for campsites ranges from $15 to $20 per night. This fee includes access to all amenities, such as restrooms, showers, and the camp store. Additional costs may apply for firewood, laundry, and shower use.

Unique Features and Scenic Views

Loft Mountain Campground offers some of the most breathtaking views in Shenandoah National Park. You'll enjoy panoramic vistas of the Shenandoah Valley and the rolling Blue Ridge Mountains right from your campsite. The campground is also close to several trailheads, including the Appalachian Trail and the Frazier Discovery Trail, providing ample opportunities for hiking and wildlife observation. The proximity to Loft Mountain Wayside offers convenient access to dining and a gift shop, enhancing your camping experience.

Mathews Arm Campground

Mathews Arm Campground is the northernmost campground in Shenandoah National Park, making it an ideal spot for visitors entering the park from the north. This campground offers a serene and well-equipped environment for both tent and RV campers, providing a perfect base for exploring the park's natural beauty.

Location/Address

Mathews Arm Campground is located at 801 Mathews Arm Entrance Road, Luray, VA 22835. It is situated at mile 22.1 on Skyline Drive, offering easy access to the park's northern attractions.

Amenities

The campground features 165 sites, many of which are available on a first-come, first-served basis. Amenities include:

- Restrooms: Flush toilets and potable water are available. Coin-operated showers are located nearby.

- Camp Store: Offers essentials such as firewood, ice, and basic groceries.

- Picnic Tables and Fire Pits: Each campsite is equipped with a picnic table, fire pit, and a bear-proof food storage locker.

- Trash Collection and Recycling: Conveniently located throughout the campground to maintain cleanliness and minimize wildlife encounters.

- Dump Station: Available for RV campers to manage waste disposal.

Contact Information

For inquiries and reservations, you can contact the campground office at 540-999-3500. Reservations can also be made online through the National Park Service website or by calling 877-444-6777.

Price Range

Campsite fees are $20 per night for standard non-electric sites. Discounts are available for holders of the America the Beautiful Pass, reducing the nightly rate to $10.

Unique Features and Scenic Views

Mathews Arm Campground is known for its proximity to several hiking trails, including the Overall Run Falls Trail, which leads to the park's tallest waterfall at 93 feet. The campground is nestled in a heavily wooded area, providing ample shade and a sense of seclusion. Wildlife sightings are common, with deer and various bird species frequently spotted around the campground. The peaceful setting and convenient access to trails make it a favorite among nature enthusiasts.

Scenic Views

The location of Mathews Arm Campground offers visitors stunning views of the Shenandoah Valley and surrounding mountains. The nearby overlooks along Skyline Drive provide panoramic vistas that are particularly breathtaking during sunrise and sunset. The campground's proximity to hiking trails ensures that you can easily immerse yourself in the park's natural beauty right from your campsite.

Lewis Mountain Campground

Lewis Mountain Campground is a charming and less-crowded option within Shenandoah National Park, perfect for those seeking a quieter camping experience. It's the smallest campground in the park, offering a more intimate setting compared to its larger counterparts.

Location/Address

You will find Lewis Mountain Campground at mile 57.5 on Skyline Drive, centrally located within the park. The physical address is 3655 U.S. Highway 211 East, Luray, VA 22835. This location is conveniently close to popular attractions like Big Meadows, just seven miles away.

Amenities

Lewis Mountain Campground provides a range of amenities to ensure a comfortable stay:

- Campsites: 30 sites suitable for tents and trailers

- Restrooms: Flush toilets

- Showers: Coin-operated hot showers

- Laundry: Coin-operated laundry facilities

- Camp Store: Seasonal store offering firewood, ice, and basic supplies

- Picnic Tables and Fire Rings: Available at each campsite

- Bear Boxes: Provided for food storage to keep wildlife at bay

- Recycling and Trash Disposal: Conveniently located within the campground.

Contact Information

For additional information or specific inquiries, you can reach out to the park:

- Phone: 540-999-3500

Price Range

The cost of camping at Lewis Mountain Campground typically ranges from $15 to $20 per night. This fee includes access to all the basic amenities such as restrooms, showers, and the camp store. Additional costs may apply for firewood, laundry, and shower usage.

Unique Features and Scenic Views

Lewis Mountain Campground offers a serene setting with fewer crowds, making it a hidden gem within Shenandoah National Park. The location provides easy access to some of the park's most popular hiking trails and scenic spots. The campground is nestled between Skyline Drive and the Appalachian Trail, offering convenient access to breathtaking views and wildlife watching. In the spring, enjoy the vibrant wildflowers, and in the fall, marvel at the stunning autumn foliage.

Practical Tips for Campers

- Plan Ahead: Make your reservations well in advance to secure your preferred site, especially during peak seasons.

- Prepare for Weather: Shenandoah's weather can be unpredictable. Pack layers to adjust to varying temperatures and conditions.

- Bear Safety: The park is home to black bears. Use bear-proof food storage and follow guidelines to keep both you and the wildlife safe.

- Noise Considerations: Some loops are generator-free for a quieter experience. Choose your site based on your preference for noise levels.

- Connectivity: Cell service can be spotty or nonexistent. Plan accordingly and enjoy the opportunity to disconnect and immerse yourself in nature.

Lodges

Skyland Lodge, Shenandoah National Park

Skyland Lodge is one of Shenandoah National Park's most renowned accommodations, offering a blend of comfort and rustic charm. Established in 1888, the lodge sits nestled at the highest point on Skyline Drive, boasting impressive views and a peaceful setting.

Location/Address

Skyland Lodge is located within Shenandoah National Park, between mile markers 41.7 and 42.5 on Skyline Drive, providing easy access to various park amenities and hiking trails. The physical address is Skyland Upper Loop, Mile 41, Luray, VA 22835.

Amenities

Skyland Lodge offers a variety of rooms and cabins, ensuring a comfortable stay in the heart of nature. Room options include traditional rooms, preferred rooms, and suites, with several pet-friendly options available. Amenities at the lodge include:

- Dining options at the Pollock Dining Room and the Mountain Taproom
- Outdoor patio dining with spectacular views
- Limited Wi-Fi access in common areas
- On-site gift shop and horseback riding services

Contact Information

For reservations and more information, you can contact Skyland Lodge directly:

- Phone: 877-847-1919

Price Range

Room rates at Skyland Lodge vary depending on the type and season, typically ranging from $192 to $284 per night. These rates reflect the premium experience and exclusive location of the lodge within the national park.

Unique Features and Scenic Views

Perched at an elevation of 3,680 feet, Skyland Lodge offers unmatched views of the Shenandoah Valley. It's an ideal spot for those looking to immerse themselves in the park's natural beauty. The lodge itself is part of the park's history, offering a vintage charm that complements its wilderness setting. Guests often enjoy sunrise or sunset views directly from their rooms or the lodge's expansive outdoor areas.

Skyland Lodge not only provides a comfortable stay but also acts as a gateway to exploring the extensive trails and natural beauty of Shenandoah National Park. Whether you're looking to hike, dine with a view, or simply relax in a historic setting, Skyland Lodge offers a memorable experience.

Big Meadows Lodge - Your Shenandoah Retreat

Big Meadows Lodge offers a unique blend of rustic charm and comfort amidst the park's captivating scenery. This lodge serves as an ideal base for exploring the park's landscapes, providing easy access to a range of outdoor activities and breathtaking vistas.

Location/Address

Situated in the heart of Shenandoah National Park, the lodge is conveniently located at Mile 51.2, Skyline Drive, Shenandoah National Park, Virginia.

Amenities

Guests at Big Meadows Lodge can enjoy a variety of amenities designed to enhance their stay:

- A variety of room types including traditional rooms, suites, and detached cabins
- Dining options at the Spottswood Dining Room and New Market Taproom
- No in-room telephones; cell service varies by carrier
- Accessibility features in designated rooms
- Seasonal operation of the lodge, generally from April 24 to November 5.

Contact Information

To inquire further or to make a reservation:

- Phone: 877-847-1919

Price Range

Room rates vary depending on the type and season, typically ranging from $154 to $285 per night. This range includes options from basic rooms to more spacious suites and cabins. The lodge offers a detailed breakdown of rates and availability on its website or through direct inquiries.

Unique Features and Scenic Views

Big Meadows Lodge is renowned not only for its accommodations but also for its spectacular views of the Shenandoah Valley and access to the Big Meadow, a large, grassy area known for its stunning vistas and wildlife viewing opportunities. The lodge's location makes it a perfect spot for stargazing and enjoying the serene environment of the park.

Lewis Mountain Cabins

Lewis Mountain Cabins provide a quaint and immersive experience in Shenandoah National Park. Perfect for families, couples, or individuals seeking a rustic retreat amidst nature, these cabins combine the comfort of basic home amenities with the charm of outdoor living.

Location/Address

Located at Mile 57.5 along the picturesque Skyline Drive in Elkton, VA, Lewis Mountain Cabins are easily accessible while offering a secluded feel deep within the park.

Amenities

Each cabin features:

- Comfortable bedding

- Electric lighting (note there's no air conditioning)

- Heating for cooler nights

- A private bathroom

- An outdoor grill pit and picnic table

Guests need to bring their own cooking supplies and food storage coolers as there is no refrigeration. Firewood is available for purchase, essential for those looking to enjoy an evening around the fire.

Contact Information

For reservations and more information, you can contact the cabins at 877-847-1919.

Price Range

Prices start at around $173 per night, varying by cabin type and season. Considering their location within the national park and the amenities offered, this provides a good value for those looking to enhance their stay in Shenandoah with a more comfortable, yet authentic experience.

Unique Features and Scenic Views

The cabins are nestled in a location that offers stunning views of the Blue Ridge Mountains, providing a perfect backdrop for a peaceful escape from the hustle and bustle of city life. The area around Lewis Mountain is known for its scenic beauty and is a great spot for wildlife watching, with frequent sightings of deer and other forest animals. The proximity to hiking trails and the Skyline Drive also means that stunning vistas and outdoor activities are just steps away.

Big Meadows Wayside

Big Meadows Wayside is more than just a place to grab a bite; it's an integral part of the Shenandoah National Park experience, providing nourishment, supplies, and a pleasant break in a scenic location. Whether you're passing through during a long hike or looking for a place to relax and enjoy the park's natural beauty, Big Meadows Wayside offers a convenient and welcoming atmosphere.

Location and Accessibility

Big Meadows Wayside, situated at mile 51.2 on Skyline Drive in Shenandoah National Park, is a popular stop for visitors seeking refreshments and supplies in a rustic setting. This location serves as a central hub within the park, providing not only food and drink but also essential camping and hiking supplies.

Amenities

The Wayside features a cafeteria-style restaurant with a variety of dining options including regional favorites, a 'Grab 'n Go' kiosk for quick snacks and meals, and a large gift shop. It also provides picnic tables for those preferring to dine outdoors amidst the park's natural beauty. For convenience, there are facilities such as restrooms and potable water, making it a comfortable stop during your park exploration.

Operating Seasons and Hours

Big Meadows Wayside operates seasonally, typically opening in late March and closing in early November. It's important to note that operating hours can vary, so checking the latest updates before your visit is recommended.

Contact Information and Reservations

While no reservations are required for dining at Big Meadows Wayside, it's a first-come, first-served facility. For more information about current services and specific inquiries, visitors can contact Delaware North, which manages the facility, through their website or by calling the dedicated phone number for Shenandoah National Park services.

Price Range

The cost at Big Meadows Wayside varies depending on the food and supplies purchased. The dining area offers meals and snacks at moderate prices, typical of national park service facilities, ensuring that all visitors have access to food and essentials during their park visit.

Unique Features

The location of Big Meadows Wayside offers stunning views of the surrounding meadows, which are especially captivating during the blooming seasons. The area is known for its vibrant wildflowers and is also a prime spot for wildlife watching, providing a picturesque backdrop for a meal or a break from hiking.

Nearby Accommodation and Camping Options

Hampton Inn Front Royal

Hampton Inn Front Royal is strategically positioned as a gateway to Shenandoah National Park, offering guests comfortable lodging with easy access to the park's numerous attractions. This hotel is ideal for visitors looking to explore the natural beauty and historical sites of the Shenandoah Valley.

Location/Address

Located at 9800 Winchester Road, Front Royal, VA 22630, Hampton Inn Front Royal sits conveniently at the intersection of Route 522 and Interstate 66. This location provides prime access to Skyline Drive and is a pivotal starting point for various local tours.

Amenities

- Free Parking: Available for all guests, making it easy to explore the region by car.

- Free High-Speed Internet (WiFi): Keeps you connected throughout your stay.

- Pool and Fitness Center: Facilities designed for relaxation and maintaining your fitness routine.

- Complimentary Breakfast: A diverse buffet that includes both hot and cold options to start your day right.

- Banquet and Meeting Facilities: Suitable for hosting a range of events and meetings.

- Convenience Store and Vending Machines: Easily accessible for snacks and essentials.

- Non-Smoking Rooms: All accommodations are non-smoking, ensuring a comfortable environment for all guests.

Contact Information

For more detailed inquiries or to make reservations, contact Hampton Inn Front Royal directly at +1 540-635-1882.

Reservation Requirements

Reservations can be made online through the hotel's website or over the phone. Early booking is recommended, particularly during peak tourism seasons, to secure your preferred room type.

Price Range

Room rates at Hampton Inn Front Royal vary depending on the season and room type. Prices are generally competitive for the area, providing good value considering the array of amenities offered.

Unique Features and Scenic Views

The hotel offers picturesque views of the Shenandoah Valley, renowned for its scenic landscapes and outdoor recreational activities. Its location provides an excellent base for exploring Skyline Drive and the surrounding areas, making it a popular choice for both leisure and business travelers.

The Wayside Inn & Larrick's Tavern

The Wayside Inn & Larrick's Tavern, established in 1797, offers a historical retreat nestled in the picturesque Shenandoah Valley in Middletown, Virginia. Renowned for its blend of rich history with modern accommodations and dining, this inn is a cherished landmark for both travelers and history enthusiasts.

Location/Address

The inn is located at 7783 Main St., Middletown, VA 22645, providing a serene setting that is easily accessible from major routes and close to local attractions.

Amenities

- Free Parking: Ample space available for guests, enhancing convenience.

- Free High-Speed Internet (WiFi): Ensures connectivity throughout your stay.

- Bar/Lounge and Restaurant: Features Larrick's Tavern, offering local cuisine and drinks.

- Children Activities: Kid and family-friendly activities are available to keep younger guests entertained.

- Meeting Rooms: Suitable for business gatherings, equipped with necessary facilities.

- ATM on Site: For easy financial transactions.

- Happy Hour and Outdoor Dining Area: Enjoy social hours and meals in a scenic outdoor setting.

- Wine/Champagne: A selection of fine beverages for guests to enjoy.

Contact Information

For inquiries and reservations, contact the inn at 540-869-1797 or via email at info@wayside1797.com. Additional details are available on their website, www.thewaysideinn1797.com, for those looking to learn more or book a stay.

Reservation Requirements

It is advisable to book in advance, particularly during peak seasons, to secure your preferred accommodation. Reservations can be made by phone or directly through the inn's website.

Price Range

Room rates are competitive, reflecting the quality of service and amenities provided.

Unique Features and Scenic Views

The Wayside Inn & Larrick's Tavern is set against the backdrop of the beautiful Shenandoah Valley, offering guests not only a place to stay but an experience steeped in history. The inn's architecture and décor reflect its long history, providing a unique and immersive atmosphere.

Sleep Inn & Suites

Sleep Inn & Suites offers a welcoming retreat in the charming town of Winchester, VA. Located less than a mile from Shenandoah University, this hotel combines convenience with comfort, making it an ideal choice for both leisure and business travelers.

Location/Address

Situated at 140 Costello Dr, Winchester, VA 22602-4306, Sleep Inn & Suites provides easy access to local attractions including historic landmarks, theme parks, and raceways, enriching your visit with a variety of experiences.

Amenities

- Free Morning Medley Hot Breakfast: Start your day with a hearty breakfast including Belgian waffles and fresh fruits.

- Indoor Heated Pool: Enjoy a swim or maintain your exercise routine in the fitness center.

- Business Center: Stay productive with high-speed internet access and business facilities.

- Tastefully Decorated Rooms: Each room features modern conveniences such as coffee makers, microwaves, refrigerators, and flat-screen TVs with cable.

- Multilingual Staff: Communicate effectively in English, Russian, and Spanish with the trained, friendly staff.

Contact Information

For more information or to make a reservation, contact Sleep Inn & Suites at +1 (540) 667-7636. You can also visit their website, www.choicehotels.com/en-uk/virginia/winchester/sleep-inn-hotels/, for online bookings and additional details.

Reservation Requirements

Advanced bookings are recommended to ensure availability, especially during peak periods or local events. Reservations can be made online, or over the phone.

Price Range

Sleep Inn & Suites offers budget-friendly accommodations without compromising on quality or comfort. The price ranges from $90 to $103.

Unique Features and Scenic Views

Located in Winchester, the hotel is in proximity to numerous cultural and historical sites, providing ample opportunities for exploration and enjoyment. Its modern amenities and family-friendly accommodations ensure a comfortable and memorable stay for all guests.

Comfort Inn Woodstock Shenandoah

Comfort Inn Woodstock Shenandoah provides a cozy retreat conveniently located just off Interstate 81 in Woodstock, VA. Positioned less than a mile from Shenandoah University, this hotel is an excellent base for both natural explorations and cultural experiences in the region.

Location/Address

You'll find the Comfort Inn Woodstock Shenandoah at 1011 Motel Dr, Woodstock, VA 22664-1022. Its strategic location near Interstate 81 facilitates easy access to local attractions and outdoor destinations.

Amenities

- Free Parking: Available to all guests, enhancing convenience during your stay.

- Free High-Speed Internet (WiFi): Keeps you connected during your travels.

- Outdoor Pool: Provides a refreshing escape from the Virginia heat.

- Fitness Center with Gym/Workout Room: Helps maintain your fitness routine.

- Free Hot Breakfast: Offers a variety of delicious options to start your day.

- Children Activities: Keeps younger guests entertained throughout their stay.

- Pet-Friendly Accommodations: Allows you to bring along your furry friends.

Contact Information

For reservations and more detailed inquiries, you can contact Comfort Inn Woodstock Shenandoah directly at +1 540-784-4004. This number provides a direct line to the hotel for booking and customer service.

Price Range

The hotel offers budget-friendly rates without compromising comfort or quality, aiming to provide good value for guests. The price ranges from $111 to $154.

Unique Features and Scenic Views

Located near key attractions like Shenandoah University and various historical sites, Comfort Inn Woodstock Shenandoah is not only a place for relaxation but also a convenient point for exploring the rich history and natural beauty of the Shenandoah Valley. Whether visiting for business or leisure, the hotel's amenities and location make it a preferred choice for travelers seeking both convenience and comfort.

Chapter 3: Exploring Nature

Wildlife Watching Opportunities

Embark on a thrilling adventure in the Shenandoah National Park, exploring and uncovering the rich and diverse wildlife that inhabits various corners of this natural paradise. Let's delve into some of the captivating wildlife-watching opportunities that await you:

Bird Watching

One of the most popular wildlife-watching activities in Shenandoah National Park is bird watching. With its diverse ecosystems and variety of habitats, the park is a haven for avian enthusiasts. As you venture along the park's trails and viewpoints, you are treated to a symphony of bird songs and the sight of colorful plumage flashing through the vibrant foliage. Among the remarkable species you may encounter are the regal bald eagles, symbolizing strength and freedom as they soar through the skies. You may also spot the brilliant flashes of warblers and tanagers, their vibrant hues adding a splash of color to the verdant landscape. Keep your binoculars at the ready-to-catch sight of elusive wood thrushes, their melodious songs adding a magical soundtrack to our explorations.

Deer and Elk Spotting

As you traverse the meadows and forests of Shenandoah National Park, a frequent sight to behold is the graceful white-tailed deer, symbols of gentle elegance and natural resilience. Rising early or venturing out near dusk increases your chances of glimpsing these majestic creatures as they emerge from their hidden sanctuaries to gracefully graze amidst their scenic surroundings. With their cautious eyes and nimble movements, the deer embodies the tranquility and vitality of the park. Additionally, in the northern areas of the park, the stately elk make occasional appearances, delighting lucky observers with their regal stature and elegant antlers that crown their heads. These encounters with wildlife remind you of the untouched wonders that exist within Shenandoah National Park.

Black Bear Encounters

For those seeking a more exhilarating wildlife experience, Shenandoah National Park offers an opportunity to encounter the elusive and awe-inspiring black bears that call this sanctuary home. These magnificent creatures, known for their strength and intelligence, are an integral part of the park's ecosystem. As you wander through the park's quiet trails and hidden corners, you may be fortunate enough to catch a glimpse of a bear foraging for food or ambling through the forest. It is important, however, to remember that bears are wild animals deserving of our respect and distance. By responsibly and ethically observing these creatures from afar, you ensure both their safety and your own, preserving the harmony between humans and wildlife.

Amphibians and Reptiles

Shenandoah National Park is a haven for amphibians and reptiles, boasting a rich variety of species. From the melodious chorus of frogs and the vibrant hues of salamanders to the intricate patterns of turtles and the slithering grace of snakes, the park's moist woodlands, streams, and meadows provide sanctuary for these fascinating creatures. As you venture into these habitats, you may come across playful frogs leaping from the undergrowth, or perhaps a shy salamander carefully navigating the forest floor. Patient observation reveals the intricate behaviors and adaptations of these creatures, reminding you of the interconnectedness of all life within this wondrous ecosystem.

Bird Watching

Insect Marvels

While often overlooked, the world of insects within Shenandoah National Park is a captivating realm waiting to be explored. From the delicate fluttering of butterflies to the gentle hum of bees and the array of colors displayed by beetles and dragonflies, insects play a vital role in maintaining the park's ecological balance. Take the time to observe their fascinating behaviors and marvel at their vibrant colors, a reminder of the intricate beauty that exists within even the smallest inhabitants of this natural sanctuary. Pause to witness the dance of butterflies as they flit between flowers, or observe the tireless work of bees pollinating the landscape, ensuring the continuation of life's delicate cycle.

Raptor Migration

Shenandoah National Park, with its diverse landscapes and open skies, serves as a crucial pathway for the annual migration of raptors. During certain times of the year, you can witness the awe-inspiring spectacle of these majestic birds of prey as they soar through the park's airspace. Keep your eyes trained on the horizon and scan the skies for the graceful silhouettes of hawks, eagles, and falcons as they undertake their incredible migratory journeys. The cliffs and overlooks within the park provide excellent vantage points to observe these magnificent creatures in action.

Wildflower and Butterfly Exploration

If you have an appreciation for the delicate beauty of wildflowers and the enchanting dances of butterflies, Shenandoah National Park won't disappoint. The park is home to numerous species of wildflowers, creating a vibrant tapestry throughout the seasons. As you stroll along the park's trails, keep an eye out for bursts of color amidst the greenery. These alluring blossoms attract a myriad of butterflies, turning the meadows and woodlands into a captivating ballet of wings and petals. Take the time to observe the intricate patterns and behaviors of these delicate creatures, immersing yourself in the wonders of nature's smallest marvels.

Owls and Nocturnal Wildlife

As the sun sets and darkness blankets Shenandoah National Park, a different world awakens. For those who embrace the mysteries of the night, nocturnal wildlife watching can unveil a realm filled with hooting owls, elusive mammals, and enchanting insects. Guided night hikes or starlit picnics can offer unique opportunities to observe creatures such as the Eastern screech-owl or the agile flying squirrels as they go about their nightly activities. Allow yourself to be captivated by the symphony of nocturnal sounds and the subtle movements that reveal the hidden wonders of the park's nocturnal inhabitants.

Stream Walks and Aquatic Wildlife

If you find solace amidst the tranquil babbling of streams and the serenity of riparian habitats, Shenandoah National Park offers the chance to explore the wonders of aquatic wildlife. Lace up your boots and embark on stream walks, where you can observe fish darting between rocks, listen to the chorus of frogs, and catch glimpses of elusive amphibians. The streams and rivers within the park provide vital habitats for a variety of aquatic creatures, adding yet another dimension to your wildlife-watching experiences.

Winter Wildlife Tracking

During the winter months, when the park is adorned in a glistening blanket of snow, a unique opportunity presents itself to hone your tracking skills and search for signs of wildlife. As you traverse the winter trails, look for footprints left by deer, rabbits, and other creatures that roam the snowy landscape. Pay attention to the subtle clues that reveal the presence of wildlife, such as nibbled twigs or feathers left behind after a predator's meal. By deciphering these tracks and signs, you can piece together a picture of the intricate lives led by the park's wildlife throughout the colder months.

Safety tips to keep in mind

It is essential to prioritize both your safety and the well-being of the animals while observing wildlife in Shenandoah National Park. Here are some important safety tips to keep in mind:

Maintain a Safe Distance

To ensure your safety and avoid causing distress to the wildlife, always maintain a safe distance. Use binoculars or a zoom lens to get a closer view without intruding upon their natural habitat. The National Park Service recommends staying at least 50 yards away from most wildlife, while it is advisable to maintain an even greater distance of at least 150 yards from bears or other potentially dangerous animals. Respecting their space is crucial for both your safety and the welfare of the wildlife.

Never Feed or Approach Wildlife

Feeding wildlife can have severe consequences for both animals and humans. It disrupts natural behaviors and can lead to dependency, aggression, and potential harm to both wildlife and people. Appreciate wildlife from afar and resist the temptation to approach or feed them. Remember, these creatures are wild and their behaviors can be unpredictable. Watch and photograph, but never touch, feed, or attempt to interact with them.

Use Caution with Bears

If you happen to encounter a bear while exploring Shenandoah National Park, it is important to handle the situation with utmost care and respect. Maintain a safe distance, never approach the bear, and try to avoid direct eye contact, as this may be perceived as a threat. If a bear notices your presence, speak in a calm and assertive voice, allowing it to identify you as a human. Slowly back away and give the bear space to move away from you. It is vital not to run or make sudden movements, as this may trigger the bear's instinct to chase. Familiarize yourself with bear safety guidelines before your visit to ensure you are well-prepared.

Stick to Designated Trails

To protect both yourself and the wildlife, it is important to stay on designated trails while exploring Shenandoah National Park. Going off-trail can disrupt habitats, harm native plants, and potentially disturb animal burrows or nesting sites. Following the established paths helps minimize your impact on the environment and preserves the integrity of the park's delicate ecosystems.

Observe Quietly and Respectfully

When observing wildlife, maintain a quiet and calm demeanor. Noise and sudden movements can startle or distress animals, possibly leading to erratic behavior or a quick retreat. Keep conversations soft and minimize any unnecessary disturbances. By being respectful and considerate, you allow both yourself and fellow visitors the opportunity to observe wildlife undisturbed, ensuring a more enjoyable and rewarding experience for all.

Be Prepared and Informed

Before embarking on your wildlife-watching adventure, familiarize yourself with park regulations and guidelines provided by the National Park Service. Seek information about any potential wildlife activity or closures in the area you plan to explore. Dress appropriately for the weather, wear proper footwear, and bring essential supplies such as water, snacks, insect repellent, and sunscreen. Additionally, carry a map or utilize a GPS device to stay oriented while exploring the park's vast terrain.

By adhering to these safety tips and guidelines, you can maximize the enjoyment of your wildlife-watching experiences in Shenandoah National Park while ensuring the well-being of the park's remarkable inhabitants and preserving the natural balance of this captivating ecosystem.

Specific regulations or guidelines You should be aware of before visiting the park

Park Hours and Entrance Fees

Shenandoah National Park is open year-round, but the operating hours may vary depending on the season. It's advisable to check the official park website or contact the park directly to confirm the current hours of operation. Additionally, there is an entrance fee to access the park, which is used for the preservation and enhancement of its resources. Make sure to review the entrance fees and payment methods before your visit.

Stay on Designated Trails and Roads

To conserve the park's ecosystems and minimize human impact, it is essential to stay on designated trails and roads. Straying off the established paths can harm fragile plant life, disturb animal habitats, and contribute to soil erosion. The park offers a wide range of trails suitable for various skill levels and preferences, so select your route accordingly and adhere to the trail guidelines.

Campfire Restrictions

To prevent the risk of wildfires, there may be restrictions on campfire usage within Shenandoah National Park. These restrictions can vary depending on factors such as weather conditions and fire danger levels. It is important to abide by these regulations and guidelines to ensure the safety of yourself and the park's surroundings. If campfires are prohibited, alternate means of cooking or heating should be used, in accordance with park rules.

Wildlife Viewing Guidelines

While observing wildlife, it's crucial to follow the guidelines that protect both you and the animals. Keep a safe distance from wildlife, typically recommended as at least 50 yards for most animals and 150 yards for potentially dangerous animals such as bears. Remember to never feed or approach wildlife, as this can disrupt their natural behaviors and pose dangers to both wildlife and humans. It is also important to adhere to specific guidelines provided for encounters with bears and other potentially hazardous animals.

Leave No Trace Principles

Shenandoah National Park promotes the Leave No Trace principles, which encourage responsible outdoor practices. These principles include disposing of waste properly, leaving natural and cultural features undisturbed, minimizing campfire impacts, respecting wildlife, and being considerate of other visitors. Familiarize yourself with these principles and strive to leave the park as you found it, preserving its pristine beauty for future generations.

Take note of these key regulations and guidelines before visiting Shenandoah National Park. It is imperative to review the official regulations provided by the National Park Service and stay informed about any temporary closures, advisories, or restrictions that may be in place during your visit. By respecting these guidelines, you can contribute to the preservation and enjoyment of this remarkable natural treasure.

Stargazing in Shenandoah National Park

As you venture into the depths of Shenandoah National Park, take a moment to pause and contemplate the awe-inspiring beauty of the night sky. Designated as a Dark Sky Park by the International Dark-Sky Association, the park's commitment to preserving the natural darkness has created an ideal haven for stargazers. Away from the bustling city lights, the unspoiled skies of Shenandoah come alive with a tapestry of stars, planets, and celestial marvels.

Preparing for Your Stargazing Adventure

Before embarking on your expedition to witness the celestial wonders of Shenandoah National Park, it is essential to come prepared. Here are some tips and considerations to make your stargazing experience unforgettable:

Checking the Weather

As you plan your stargazing adventure, consult the weather forecast to ensure clear skies and optimal visibility. Cloud cover and atmospheric conditions can greatly affect the visibility of stars and celestial objects. Choose a night when the forecast predicts minimal cloud cover, allowing the stars to shine at their brightest.

Dressing for the Occasion

Shenandoah's nights can be quite cool, even during the summer months. As you embark on your stargazing journey, remember to dress in layers to stay comfortable throughout the night. Bring a warm jacket, hat, and gloves to ward off the chill that accompanies the darkness. Additionally, comfortable shoes and a blanket or camping chair will enhance your overall experience.

Finding the Perfect Spot

To fully immerse yourself in the celestial wonders, venture away from artificial lights. Seek out locations with unobstructed views and minimal light pollution, such as meadows or overlooks. Popular stargazing spots in Shenandoah National Park include Hawksbill Summit, Skyline Drive, and the scenic Big Meadows area. Each of these locations offers expansive vistas that provide an ideal canvas for stargazing.

Timing is Everything

The best time to observe the wonders of the night sky can vary depending on the moon's phase and its rise and set times. To maximize your stargazing experience, plan your visit during a new moon or crescent moon phase when the skies are darkest. During these phases, the absence of moonlight allows for optimal visibility of stars and celestial objects. Consult astronomical charts or local resources to determine the moon phase during your visit.

Exploring the Celestial Delights

As you step into the vast expanse of the Shenandoah night sky, prepare to be mesmerized by the celestial ballet unfolding above you. Here are some notable highlights and celestial phenomena to observe during your stargazing adventure:

Star Clusters

Look to the heavens and immerse yourself in the vastness of star clusters. With the naked eye, you can observe clusters such as the Pleiades (also known as the Seven Sisters) and the famous Beehive Cluster (Messier 44). These clusters are comprised of hundreds or even thousands of stars and offer a spectacular sight when observed through binoculars or a telescope.

Planetary Dance

Shenandoah National Park offers an exceptional opportunity to witness our neighboring planets in the night sky. Keep an eye out for Jupiter, Saturn, and Mars as they make their journey across the celestial stage. With the help of a telescope or even a good pair of binoculars, you can observe the cloud bands of Jupiter, the magnificent rings of Saturn, and the reddish hues of Mars.

The Milky Way

One of the most awe-inspiring sights in the night sky is our galaxy, the Milky Way. In Shenandoah National Park's dark skies, the Milky Way reveals itself as a luminous band stretching from one horizon to the other. Find a spot away from city lights, lie back, and let the Milky Way guide your imagination into the depths of the universe.

Meteor Showers

Shenandoah National Park provides a front-row seat to meteor showers throughout the year. During these celestial events, shooting stars streak across the sky, leaving trails of light in their wake. Keep an eye on meteor shower calendars and plan your visit accordingly to witness the Perseids, Geminids, and other meteor showers that grace the night sky.

Constellations

Take a journey through ancient mythology as you explore the constellations that adorn the Shenandoah night sky. Hercules, Orion,

Ursa Major (the Great Bear), and other famous constellations can be easily identified and traced across the canvas of stars. Enhance your stargazing experience by familiarizing yourself with the patterns and stories behind these iconic constellations.

Recommended Equipment for Stargazing

To make the most of your stargazing adventure in Shenandoah National Park, consider bringing along the following equipment:

Binoculars

A pair of binoculars can greatly enhance your celestial observations. Opt for binoculars with a larger aperture, such as 7x50 or 10x50, which allow for better light-gathering capabilities and a wider field of view. They are lightweight, easy to use, and can bring distant celestial objects into clearer focus.

Telescope

If you're eager to delve deeper into the realms of the night sky, consider investing in a telescope. A telescope will provide you with a closer and more detailed view of celestial objects, allowing you to explore the moon's craters, study the bands of Jupiter, and marvel at the rings of Saturn. Look for a telescope with sufficient aperture size and consider a portable and easy-to-use model for your stargazing adventures in the park.

Star Chart or Mobile Apps

A star chart or mobile app can serve as your navigational guide through the night sky. These tools will help you identify constellations, locate planets, and spot significant celestial objects. Popular apps like SkyView, Star Walk, and Stellarium provide real-time information and can help you make the most of your stargazing experience.

Remember, while equipment can enhance your observation, the naked eye is a wonderful tool for stargazing. Take time to simply lay back and appreciate the brilliance of the stars.

Thus, as you ignite your curiosity and embark on a journey through the vast expanse of Shenandoah National Park's pristine night sky, let the wonders of the cosmos guide your imagination. From star clusters to planetary dances, the celestial delights of Shenandoah National Park offer a humbling and mesmerizing experience. Take a moment to immerse yourself in the majesty of the night sky, and may your stargazing adventure in Shenandoah National Park be filled with awe, wonder, and a deeper connection to the universe.

Chapter 4: Outdoor Adventures

Top Hiking Trails for All Levels

Easy Trails

Limberlost Trail

If you're seeking a leisurely hike that allows you to fully appreciate the beauty of Shenandoah's natural surroundings without exerting too much effort, the Limberlost Trail is an ideal choice. This gentle, 1.3-mile loop trail immerses you in the tranquility of the park, offering a captivating journey through dense foliage, towering trees, and an enchanting meandering stream.

Located in the Central District of Shenandoah National Park, the Limberlost Trail is easily accessible and provides a delightful introduction to the park's flora and fauna. This trail is suitable for hikers of all ages and is wheelchair accessible, making it an inclusive experience for all visitors.

As you begin your adventure on the Limberlost Trail, you will be greeted by a well-maintained path that winds its way through a lush forest. The trail is shaded by a canopy of ancient trees, ensuring a pleasant hiking experience even on warm summer days.

The Limberlost Trail showcases the rich biodiversity of Shenandoah National Park, offering glimpses of vibrant wildflowers, ferns, and mosses that adorn the forest floor. Take your time to observe the delicate beauty of these plant species and appreciate the intricate balance of nature that surrounds you.

One of the highlights of the Limberlost Trail is the Limberlost Interpretive Loop, a short side trail that provides educational signage and interactive exhibits. These informative displays offer insights into the park's ecosystem, wildlife, and the importance of preserving this pristine wilderness. Take a moment to pause and engage with these exhibits, deepening your understanding and connection to the natural wonders of Shenandoah.

As you continue along the trail, you will encounter the gentle babbling of Limberlost Brook. This serene stream adds to the peaceful atmosphere and offers a refreshing respite amidst the verdant surroundings. Listen to the soothing sounds of the water as it cascades over rocks and meanders through the forest, and perhaps even dip your feet in to cool off on hot summer days.

Wildlife enthusiasts will appreciate the Limberlost Trail's potential for wildlife sightings. Be watchful as you wander the path, as you may catch a glimpse of white-tailed deer quietly grazing, or a variety of bird species fluttering from branch to branch. Binoculars can enhance your chances of spotting forest dwellers such as woodpeckers, warblers, and owls. Remember to remain quiet and respectful, allowing the creatures to thrive undisturbed in their natural habitat.

Along the trail, strategically placed benches invite you to pause, rest, and soak in the beauty that surrounds you. Take the opportunity to relax and reflect, breathing in the crisp mountain air and allowing the tranquility of the wilderness to rejuvenate your spirit.

The Limberlost Trail also offers excellent photographic opportunities. Capture the interplay of light and shadow as the sun filters through the trees, illuminating the forest floor. Feel free to immortalize the vibrant colors of the wildflowers or the delicate patterns of the moss-covered rocks that line the path. Remember to be mindful of any photography restrictions and always prioritize the well-being of the natural environment.

As you near the end of the Limberlost Trail, you will complete the loop, arriving back at the trailhead where your adventure began. Take a moment to reflect on the natural wonders you have witnessed and the tranquility you have experienced. The Limberlost Trail provides a serene introduction to the breathtaking beauty that awaits you within Shenandoah National Park.

Dark Hollow Falls

Are you ready to behold the captivating beauty of one of Shenandoah National Park's hidden gems? Dark Hollow Falls, nestled in the heart of the park's Central District, offers a scenic and manageable adventure that showcases the wonders of nature. This enchanting trail winds its way through majestic forests and leads you to a mesmerizing waterfall, creating an experience that will leave you breathless.

To begin your expedition, make your way to the Dark Hollow Falls trailhead, conveniently located along Skyline Drive. As you embark on the journey, you'll find yourself surrounded by lush greenery, towering trees, and the serene sounds of nature. Take a deep breath, inhaling the crisp mountain air, as you set foot on the well-maintained path that leads you deeper into the captivating wilderness.

The Dark Hollow Falls trail spans approximately 1.4 miles, providing an enjoyable and leisurely hike suitable for hikers of all ages and fitness levels. Along the way, you'll find the trail to be moderately shaded, protecting you from the sun's rays and providing a cool and comfortable environment for your adventure.

As you progress along the trail, be prepared to witness the enchanting beauty that awaits you at every turn. The melodious songs of woodland birds fill the air, serenading you as you traverse the forested trail. Keep your eyes peeled for the occasional glimpse of wildlife, such as white-tailed deer gracefully observing your progress from a distance.

In anticipation of your final destination, the trail gradually descends through the verdant forest. Delicate sunlight filters through the canopy, casting dappled shadows on the path as you make your way closer to Dark Hollow Falls. The sound of rushing water grows louder, resonating within you, building excitement and anticipation as you approach the cascading wonder.

As you round the final bend, the magnificent Dark Hollow Falls comes into view, revealing its mesmerizing beauty with an awe-inspiring 70-foot drop. The waterfall, an epitome of natural splendor, captivates the senses with its torrential cascade. As you bask in the glory of this remarkable creation, take a moment to appreciate the tranquil ambiance and the invigorating mist that surrounds you.

The viewing area near Dark Hollow Falls offers the perfect vantage point to soak in the scenery and capture photographs that immortalize the moment. Find a comfortable spot on one of the nearby rocks, embrace the soothing sound of rushing water, and let the peacefulness of the surroundings wash over you.

If you desire a closer encounter with Dark Hollow Falls, follow the descending trail that leads you to the base of the waterfall. Exercise caution as you navigate the slightly steeper terrain, which may be slippery at times. The reward for your efforts is the chance to feel the refreshing mist on your face and witness the raw power of the cascading water. Embrace the magical energy of Dark Hollow Falls, an experience that will stay with you long after your journey concludes.

After savoring the beauty of Dark Hollow Falls, retrace your steps and make your way back to the trailhead. As you ascend the trail, take the opportunity to revel in the tranquility of the forest once more. The return journey offers a new perspective, allowing you to truly appreciate the magnificence of the natural world that surrounds you.

South River Falls

Allow me to take you on a hike that combines captivating beauty, tranquility, and a breathtaking waterfall. The South River Falls Trail, a scenic gem nestled within Shenandoah National Park, invites adventurers of all levels to immerse themselves in the stunning wilderness and witness the majesty of a cascading waterfall, creating memories that will last a lifetime.

To begin your journey, make your way to the South River Picnic Area, where you will find the trailhead waiting to guide you on your picturesque adventure. As you set foot on the well-marked path, prepare to be enchanted by the surrounding natural splendor, the melodious symphony of bird songs, and the invigorating scent of the forest.

The South River Falls Trail spans approximately 4.4 miles roundtrip, offering ample opportunity to soak in the beauty of Shenandoah National Park at a leisurely pace. The trail meanders alongside the tranquil South River, providing stunning panoramic views of the surrounding landscape. The easy incline of the trail caters to hikers of all levels, ensuring a comfortable and enjoyable adventure for all.

As you venture deeper into the woodland, a harmonious blend of sunlight and shade envelops you. Towering trees create a canopy overhead, offering respite from the sun's rays while allowing nature's light to dance through the leaves, casting enchanting shadows on your path. Take a moment to appreciate the diverse flora that adorns the surroundings - vibrant wildflowers, moss-covered rocks, and ferns that carpet the forest floor.

The melodious sounds of birdsong provide a whimsical soundtrack to your journey, captivating your senses as you progress along the trail. Keep an eye out for the occasional wildlife sighting, as Shenandoah National Park is home to a variety of creatures both grand and small. White-tailed deer may gracefully cross your path, or squirrels may playfully scamper through the branches above, adding to the charm of your experience.

With every step forward, the rhythmic sound of cascading water grows louder, foreshadowing the grand spectacle that awaits. As the trail unfolds, you'll find yourself standing on the precipice of South River Falls, a magnificent 83-foot waterfall that captivates the senses. The power and beauty of the waterfall are truly awe-inspiring, as the water plunges into a picturesque gorge, creating a mesmerizing display of nature's artistry.

Take a moment to absorb the beauty of South River Falls from the designated viewing area. Marvel at the mist that rises from the waterfall, creating a refreshing and invigorating atmosphere. The panoramic vista stretches before you, allowing you to embrace the grandeur of the surrounding wilderness while listening to the symphony of water crashing against the rocks below.

For those seeking a closer encounter with the falls, a spur trail leads you to an overlook platform that provides a unique perspective. As you approach the platform, prepare to witness the raw power and grandeur of South River Falls up close. Feel the mist on your face, hear the thunderous roar of the water, and appreciate the intricate details of the cascading flow.

After immersing yourself in the magnificence of South River Falls, retrace your steps along the trail, taking a moment to bid farewell to the wilderness that has captivated and inspired you. Embrace the simplicity and serenity of the forest, basking in the tranquility around you, as you make your way back to the trailhead.

Jones Run Falls Trailhead

Prepare to embark on a journey of tranquility and enchantment as we delve deep into the heart of Shenandoah National Park on the Jones Run Falls Trail. With its easy terrain and breathtaking views, this trail is perfect for hikers seeking a leisurely adventure amidst nature's wonder.

Begin your exploration at the Jones Run Falls Trailhead, conveniently situated in the southern reaches of Shenandoah National Park. As you step onto the well-marked path, a sense of anticipation and tranquility envelops you, leaving the hustle and bustle of everyday life behind.

The Jones Run Falls Trail spans approximately 3.2 miles round-trip, offering hikers of all levels an opportunity to bask in the captivating beauty that surrounds them. The trail meanders through a lush forest, enveloping you in a tranquil world of greenery and serenity. The gentle incline and well-maintained path make it an ideal choice for families, beginners, or those seeking a peaceful escape from the demands of everyday life.

As you make your way along the trail, take a moment to revel in the symphony of nature's sounds that surround you. The melodic songs of woodland birds fill the air, providing a whimsical accompaniment to your journey. Keep your eyes peeled for glimpses of wildlife, such as squirrels scurrying along tree branches or deer gracefully grazing in the distance. Shenandoah National Park is teeming with life, and the Jones Run Falls Trail allows you to witness the wonders of the natural world up close.

As you continue along the trail, you'll find yourself mesmerized by the lushness of the forest. Towering trees cast dappled shadows on the path, offering respite from the sun's warmth and creating a serene and inviting atmosphere. The scent of pine and earth permeates the air, filling your senses, and beckoning you deeper into the wilderness.

The highlight of the Jones Run Falls Trail emerges as you approach the stunning Jones Run Falls. Prepare for a moment of awe-inspiring beauty as the sound of cascading water grows louder with each step. As you round a bend in the trail, the majestic 42-foot waterfall comes into view, gracefully pouring into a tranquil pool below. The sight of water shimmering and glistening in the sunlight is nothing short of magical.

Take a moment to absorb the beauty that surrounds you at the designated overlook area. Let the mist from the falls cool your face as you revel in the serenity of the moment. The hypnotic sound of the rushing water washes away all worries, leaving you in a state of pure tranquility. This is nature's invitation to pause, reflect, and find peace amidst the chaos of the world.

For those seeking a closer encounter with Jones Run Falls, there is an option to descend a steep but manageable path that leads you to the base of this natural wonder. Approach with caution and take your time, as the rocks can be slippery. Once at the base, you'll not only feel the power of the water but also witness the intricate details of the falls up close. Allow yourself to be enveloped in its presence, feeling its energy and truly connecting with nature.

After fully immersing yourself in the beauty of Jones Run Falls, it's time to retrace your steps and make your way back to the trailhead. Take this opportunity to savor the peaceful ambiance of the forest, to feel the ground beneath your feet, and to appreciate the gentle rustle of leaves in the breeze. As you bid farewell to this enchanting trail, remember to carry with you the tranquility and serenity it has bestowed upon you.

Lewis Falls Trail

Imagine immersing yourself in the serenity of the forest, with soft sunbeams casting a warm glow through the towering trees, and the melodious sounds of birdsong filling the air. This is the essence of the Lewis Falls Trail, an easy hiking adventure nestled within the heart of Shenandoah National Park. Lace up your hiking boots and get ready to embark on a breathtaking journey that will leave you in awe of the natural wonders that await.

To begin your expedition, follow the signs that lead you to the Lewis Falls Trailhead. This well-marked entry point is easily accessible, providing a convenient starting point for hikers of all levels. As you set foot on the trail, a sense of anticipation builds within you, fueled by the promise of the extraordinary sights that lie ahead.

The Lewis Falls Trail spans approximately 3.3 miles round-trip, offering a leisurely and invigorating experience for outdoor enthusiasts. The trail gently winds its way through a lush forest, where old-growth trees stand tall, their branches reaching toward the sky like nature's sentinels. The well-maintained path ensures a comfortable and enjoyable hike, allowing you to fully immerse yourself in the natural beauty that surrounds you.

As you journey deeper into the wilderness, you'll find yourself enveloped by the peacefulness of the forest. The earthy scent of pine fills the air, mingling with the sweet aroma of wildflowers that dot the landscape. Take a moment to absorb the beauty that surrounds you - the vibrant colors of the blooming flora, the gentle rustle of leaves underfoot, and the soft murmurs of the wind through the trees.

The Lewis Falls Trail offers a serene escape from the noise of the modern world. As you make your way along the tranquil path, allow yourself to become attuned to the rhythmic sounds of nature. The symphony of birdsong echoes through the woods as if harmonizing with the rustling of leaves in the breeze. Keep your eyes peeled for wildlife sightings, as Shenandoah National Park is teeming with a variety of creatures. You may catch a glimpse of a white-tailed deer gracefully wandering through the undergrowth or encounter the curious scampering of a squirrel in search of its next meal.

As the trail gradually leads you closer to Lewis Falls, a sense of anticipation and wonder fills the air. The gentle rush of water grows louder with each step, foreshadowing the marvel that awaits. And then, as if by magic, the majestic Lewis Falls comes into view. The cascade of water tumbling over rocks creates a mesmerizing spectacle that captures your attention and leaves you breathless.

Take a moment to marvel at the grandeur of Lewis Falls from the designated viewing area. Stand in awe as the water crashes against the rocks, creating a symphony of sound that reverberates through the canyon. Witness the mist rising from the waters as if inviting you to come closer and feel its refreshing touch. Capture this precious moment with your camera, allowing the beauty of Lewis Falls to be forever preserved in your memories.

For those seeking a more immersive experience, there is an option to descend a short, well-maintained spur trail that leads to the base of Lewis Falls. Exercise caution as you navigate the path and be mindful of rocks that may be slippery. As you approach the base, prepare to be enveloped in the raw power and beauty of the falls. Feel the mist on your skin, hear the thunderous roar of water cascading, and be humbled by the sheer magnitude of nature's creation.

As your visit to Lewis Falls draws to a close, follow the trail back, pausing to say goodbye to the captivating forest that has sparked your sense of exploration. As you journey back to the trailhead, take a moment to ponder the tranquility that nature has gifted you. In this instance, you're reminded of the significance of safeguarding and treasuring the natural marvels that bless our world.

Mary's Rock Summit

Imagine a picturesque trail that effortlessly blends nature's beauty with an accessible journey. Enter Mary's Rock Summit Trail, a delightful escape within the enchanting embrace of Shenandoah National Park. Whether you're a seasoned hiker seeking a stroll or a beginner adventurer, this easy trail offers a captivating experience for all.

Begin your adventure at the Thornton Gap Entrance Station, where the trailhead patiently beckons you forward. The path unfolds gently, introducing you to the wonders that await in this unique corner of the park. Each step reveals a vibrant tapestry of fauna and flora, creating a symphony of colors and scents that dance upon the breeze.

As you amble along the trail, you'll feel the cares of the world melt away, replaced by a sense of peace and serenity. The soothing sounds of birdsong accompany your journey, harmonizing with the rustling leaves to create a melody that soothes your soul. The dappled sunlight filters through the towering trees, casting a gentle glow upon your path.

Prepare to be astounded as you ascend Mary's Rock, for breathtaking vistas await you at the summit. Though the trail may be easy, the rewards are no less extraordinary. As you reach the peak, pause to catch your breath and let your eyes wander across the vast expanse of Shenandoah National Park.

From Mary's Rock, witness a panorama that encompasses rolling mountains, lush forests, and the winding bends of the Shenandoah River. The grandeur of nature unfolds before you, painting a picture that words can scarcely capture. Take a moment to absorb the majesty of this scene, allowing it to seep into your being and remind you of the boundless beauty of the natural world.

As you descend from the summit, tread lightly, for it is in these quiet moments that nature's hidden treasures reveal themselves. Keep a watchful eye for the delicate wildflowers that dot the trail's edge, their colors transforming the path into a living canvas. Savor the peaceful atmosphere that envelops you, taking in the subtle whispers of the wind as it weaves through the trees.

When your journey nears its end, reminisce upon the memories you've created along this gentle trail. The sense of accomplishment, the connection with nature, and the rejuvenation of your spirit are all invaluable treasures earned through your exploration. As you bid farewell to Mary's Rock Summit, carry these experiences with you, forging a lasting bond with Shenandoah National Park.

Moderate Trails

Overall Run Falls

Nestled within the heart of Shenandoah National Park lies the mesmerizing beauty of Overall Run Falls, an intermediate hiking trail that effortlessly combines adventure and tranquility. As you set foot upon the well-worn path, prepare to be captivated by stunning vistas, the soothing gush of water, and a sense of accomplishment that comes from conquering the terrain.

The Overall Run Falls trail boasts a moderate level of difficulty, making it an ideal choice for those seeking a slightly more challenging hiking experience. The 6.4-mile round-trip adventure will lead you through a picturesque landscape that showcases the natural wonders of Shenandoah National Park.

As you embark on this invigorating journey, the trail envelops you in a lush tapestry of fauna and flora. The scent of wildflowers fills the air, as their vibrant colors adorn the landscape, creating a delightful contrast against the serene backdrop of the forest. Allow the melody of birdsong and the rustling of leaves underfoot to serenade you on this poetic hike.

The path gradually ascends, offering panoramic views that will leave you breathless at every turn. Take a moment to absorb the picturesque vistas that stretch out before you, rewarding your efforts with nature's breathtaking spectacle. The rolling mountains, velvety meadows, and cascading streams that intertwine harmoniously invite you to pause and appreciate the beauty of Shenandoah National Park.

Your anticipation grows as the sound of rushing water beckons you closer to Overall Run Falls. The gurgling chorus grows louder as you approach, heightening your excitement for the marvel that lies ahead. Following the twists and turns of the trail, you'll discover yourself standing before the majestic and awe-inspiring Overall Run Falls.

The cascading waters plunge down the cliffs, creating a hypnotic display of nature's power. Stand in wonder as the mist dances on your cheeks, refreshing your spirit and reminding you of the intricate balance of the natural world. Take a moment to immerse yourself completely in this serene oasis, allowing the symphony of water and wind to transport you to a place of tranquility.

For those longing for a closer encounter with the falls, a short spur trail descends to the base of Overall Run Falls. While the path may be slightly rugged and uneven, the rewards are immeasurable. Approach with caution as you navigate the terrain, taking care to savor each step and admire the hidden gems along the way. As you arrive at the base, the thunderous roar of water and the cool mist upon your skin will leave an indelible mark on your memory.

As your time at Overall Run Falls draws to a close, retrace your steps back along the trail, bidding a fond farewell to the splendor that has enthralled you. The journey back will offer new perspectives and ample opportunities to appreciate the grandeur of Shenandoah National Park one last time. As you reach the trailhead, take a moment to reflect on the memories that have been etched in your heart, for it is through these adventures that we discover the hidden wonders of our world.

Cedar Run Trail

Prepare yourself for an exhilarating hike along the Cedar Run Trail, where the perfect balance of serenity and excitement awaits. This moderate trail winds through the heart of Shenandoah National Park, showcasing its rugged beauty and providing a memorable experience for adventurers of varying skill levels.

Embark on your journey at the Hawksbill Gap parking area, where the trailhead eagerly awaits your arrival. As you set foot on the path, the gentle rustling of leaves underfoot accompanies you, immersing you in the tranquility of nature. Tall trees create a cool and refreshing atmosphere, shielding you from the sun's rays as you forge ahead.

The Cedar Run Trail meanders alongside a crystal-clear mountain stream, serenading you with the soothing sounds of flowing water. As you follow the path, bask in the enchantment of the surrounding forest, where lush greenery and vibrant wildflowers paint a whimsical tapestry that seems straight out of a storybook.

Throughout your hike, be prepared for occasional steep and rocky sections that will test your balance and agility. The trail challenges you, rewarding your efforts with breathtaking vistas and unforgettable encounters with nature.

As you ascend, the sound of cascading water grows louder, signaling the approach of a natural wonder – the magnificent Cedar Run Falls. A roaring display of water plunges into a pool below, creating a mesmerizing spectacle that leaves you in awe of nature's raw power. Take a moment to savor this captivating scene, feeling the cool mist on your face as you reflect on the wonders you've witnessed.

Continuing along the Cedar Run Trail, the elevation change offers panoramic views of the surrounding mountains, their summits touched by ethereal clouds. These vast vistas remind you of the expansive beauty that lies beyond, inspiring a sense of adventure and urging you to explore further.

The trail's scenic backdrop, combined with its invigorating challenges, beckons your inner explorer to push forward. Traverse wooden footbridges, navigate stone steps and cross babbling brooks. Each obstacle conquered brings a sense of accomplishment and propels you toward the next captivating discovery.

As your journey nears its end, the memories of the Cedar Run Trail will stay with you for a lifetime. The sense of adventure, the connection with nature, and the camaraderie shared among fellow hikers will forever be etched in your heart. Shenandoah National Park has presented you with a gift, and the Cedar Run Trail is merely one of its many treasures.

Remember to equip yourself with sturdy footwear, comfortable clothing, and ample water to stay hydrated throughout your hike. It's always wise to check weather conditions beforehand and pack essentials such as sunscreen, a hat, and bug repellent to ensure a comfortable and enjoyable experience.

Challenging Trails

Whiteoak Canyon and Cedar Run Circuit

If you yearn for an invigorating hiking experience that pushes the boundaries of your endurance, then look no further than the Whiteoak Canyon and Cedar Run Circuit. This challenging trail is a captivating fusion of rugged terrain and breathtaking natural beauty that can only be found within the depths of Shenandoah National Park.

Once you embark on this 9.2-mile circuit, be prepared for a grand adventure that will test your physical and mental fortitude. The trail graces you with an array of rewards, including the majestic Whiteoak Canyon Falls and the soothing serenade of Cedar Run. Lace up your sturdiest hiking boots and embrace the invigorating challenge that awaits.

As you venture forth, you'll find yourself immersed in the wild beauty of the forest. The trail meanders through towering old-growth trees, casting a verdant canopy overhead that filters the sunlight, creating delightful interplays of light and shadow. The earthy scent of moss and damp undergrowth fills the air, and the hushed whisper of the wind adds a touch of mystique to your journey.

Prepare to be captivated by the symphony of nature as you hike alongside the cascading Cedar Run. The rushing waters beckon you forward, their rhythm echoing through the dense foliage. As you navigate the rocky terrain, be mindful of your footing, as the trail presents occasional challenges that require both skill and concentration.

Soon, Whiteoak Canyon Falls comes into view, a majestic display of nature's power and beauty. The falls cascade down a series of seven tiers, their crystalline waters glistening in the sunlight. Take a moment to absorb the awe-inspiring view, the sheer height and grandeur of the falls reminding you of the raw magnificence of the natural world. Take care not to get too close, as the rocks can be treacherously slippery.

Refreshed by the enchantment of Whiteoak Canyon Falls, continue your journey along the circuit, ascending to higher elevations. The trail rewards you with awe-inspiring vistas of the surrounding mountains, where the rolling peaks stretch out as far as the eye can see. Pause for a moment to catch your breath and savor the panoramic views, a reminder of your adventurous spirit and determination.

Throughout the trail, you'll encounter stream crossings that add an extra element of excitement to your trek. Carefully navigate the stepping stones and fallen logs, ensuring your balance remains steady as you cross the crystal-clear waters. These watery interludes serve as a reminder of the untamed beauty that lies around every corner, captivating your senses and urging you forward.

As you near the end of the circuit, be prepared for a final descent that puts your endurance to the test. Your muscles may ache, and your breathing may quicken, but the exhilaration of conquering the trail will fuel your determination. With each step, you'll feel a sense of accomplishment washing over you, as you witness firsthand the rewards that await those who dare to embrace the challenges of the outdoors.

Old Rag Mountain

As you embark upon the Old Rag Mountain Trail, you are about to engage in a true test of physical and mental endurance. Known for its demanding nature, this trail draws hikers from far and wide who are willing to embrace the adventure that lies ahead.

To begin your journey, make your way to the Old Rag Parking Area, where a small fee grants you access to the trailhead. As you take your first steps onto the path, a sense of anticipation and excitement fills the air. The trail starts gently, allowing you to warm up and acclimate to the surroundings.

The landscape gradually changes as you venture deeper into this rugged wilderness. The trail meanders through a dense forest, where ancient trees stand as silent witnesses to the passage of time. With each step, you'll feel the earth beneath your feet and the whisper of nature's secrets beckoning you forward.

As the trail proceeds, it unveils a series of challenging rock scrambles that will test your agility and mental fortitude. These gripping sections require you to maneuver through crevices, over boulders, and along narrow ridges. While daunting, each obstacle conquered brings a sense of accomplishment that fuels your determination to press on.

One particularly exhilarating feature of the Old Rag Mountain Trail is the famed "Rock Scramble." Here, you'll find yourself navigating through a maze of colossal granite boulders, using both wit and strength to find your way. As you climb, crawl, and occasionally squeeze through tight spaces, the adrenaline coursing through your veins blends with the anticipation of what lies ahead.

Eventually, the rocky labyrinth leads you to the summit of Old Rag Mountain. Pause and savor the moment; for you are now standing at an elevation of 3,291 feet, surrounded by panoramic views that stretch as far as the eye can see. Drink in the stunning vistas of the Shenandoah Valley, with its rolling hills and meandering rivers, creating a tapestry of natural splendor.

Once you've caught your breath and absorbed the awe-inspiring beauty, take a moment to explore the summit's sprawling expanse. Find a comfortable spot to rest and savor a well-deserved snack, all while reveling in the knowledge that you have conquered Old Rag Mountain, a testament to your strength and determination.

But the adventure doesn't end at the summit. Prepare yourself for an equally rewarding descent that leads you through a different side of the mountain. The trail winds its way down, offering serene forest paths amidst the tranquil beauty of Shenandoah National Park. As you make your way back to the trailhead, reflect on the challenges you've overcome and the memories you've created.

Stony Man Mountain

To begin your journey, head to the Skyland Resort, nestled in the heart of Shenandoah National Park. From there, follow the signs to the Stony Man Trailhead. As you set foot on the well-marked path, you'll immediately be greeted by a gentle ascent through a lush forest. The trail snakes its way upward, unveiling mesmerizing glimpses of the scenery that lies in wait.

As you trek along, make note of the park's diverse flora and fauna. Observe the vibrant wildflowers that line the path, offering bursts of color against the backdrop of verdant greenery. Listen to the chorus of birdsong overhead, filling the air with their melodious tunes. Shenandoah National Park is a haven for nature lovers, and the journey to Stony Man Mountain is an opportunity to immerse yourself in its wonders.

As the trail progresses, it begins a gradual incline, preparing you for the challenge that lies ahead. The path meanders through rocky outcroppings, offering occasional glimpses of the sprawling Shenandoah Valley below. Feel the thrill as you ascend higher, with the anticipation of the breathtaking views that await you at the summit.

One of the highlights of the Stony Man Mountain Trail is the dramatic overlook that greets you near the top. Rest your weary legs on the ample boulders that surround the overlook, and take a moment to catch your breath. Look out over the rolling hills, forests, and shimmering rivers that make Shenandoah National Park so enchanting. It's a vista that seems to stretch for eternity, captivating both the eyes and the soul.

But the adventure doesn't end there. Beyond the overlook, the trail continues along the ridgeline, inviting further exploration. Wander along the rocky edges, marveling at the sheer cliffs that define Stony Man Mountain. Breathe in the crisp mountain air, allowing the beauty of the landscape to seep deep into your being.

As you begin your descent, reflect on the satisfaction of conquering Stony Man Mountain. The memories you've created and the challenges you've overcome will forever remain etched in your heart. This trail is not just a physical journey but also a spiritual one, as the grandeur of nature touches your soul and reminds you of the vastness of the world.

After your hiking adventure, treat yourself to a well-deserved rest. Head back to Skyland Resort, where you can relax in the cozy atmosphere and indulge in delicious meals served at their on-site dining establishments. Take a moment to exchange stories with fellow hikers and revel in the camaraderie of like-minded adventurers.

South River Falls

Begin your journey by making your way to the South River Picnic Area, a serene starting point for your hike. Here, you'll find ample parking and facilities to prepare yourself for the adventure that lies ahead. Lace up your boots, adjust your backpack, and let the trail lead you through a landscape of enchantment.

The South River Falls Trail begins with a gentle descent, guiding you through a picturesque forest boasting an abundance of lush greenery and delicate wildflowers. Feel the cool breeze brush against your face as rays of sunlight filter through the canopy above, creating a magical ambiance. The symphony of birdsong serves as nature's soundtrack, accompanying you on your peaceful journey.

As the trail meanders along the South River, you'll catch glimpses of the crystal-clear water flowing gently downstream. Take a moment to soak in the serenity and appreciate the harmonious blend of nature's elements. The river, a symphony of movement and tranquility, invites you to pause and breathe in the wonders that surround you.

As you continue to follow the trail, the sounds of rushing water grow louder, signaling your approach to the main attraction—South River Falls. The path gradually ascends, leading you to an overlook that reveals a breathtaking vista of the majestic falls cascading down the rocky cliffs. Behold the power and grace of nature's masterpiece as water plummets into the depths below, creating a mesmerizing display. Let the awe-inspiring sight rejuvenate your spirit and ignite a sense of wonder.

For a more immersive experience, descend from the overlook to the base of the falls, where a serene pool awaits. Feel the cool mist caress your skin, and listen to the symphony of water crashing against the rocks. Take a moment to reflect on the raw beauty of the natural world, and perhaps find a peaceful spot to sit and embrace the serenity surrounding you.

Once you've fully embraced the magic of South River Falls, retrace your steps back to the trailhead. As you bid farewell to this tranquil haven, carry with you the memories of a journey that blended adventure, beauty, and peace in perfect harmony.

Bearfence Mountain

As you arrive at the trailhead, located in the heart of Shenandoah National Park, the anticipation builds. Bearfence Mountain offers a truly unique hiking experience, presenting you with the opportunity to scramble up rocky cliffs and climb to the summit, where stunning panoramic views await.

The Bearfence Mountain Trail begins with a gentle ascent, leading you through a dense forest ablaze with vibrant hues of green. The trail snakes its way through towering trees, creating a cool, shaded pathway. As you make your way further, the terrain gradually changes, and you'll soon find yourself confronted with rock formations that hint at the exhilarating challenge ahead.

The trail becomes steeper, and the forest gives way to a rugged and rocky terrain. It is here that the true adventure of Bearfence Mountain begins. As you approach the first of many rock scrambles, take a moment to assess the route ahead. Using your hands and feet, navigate the exhilarating ascent, carefully placing each step to gain a foothold on the rocks. This unique experience requires focus, balance, and an adventurous spirit.

As you ascend, the landscape begins to unfold, revealing stunning vistas that will leave you breathless. Embrace the sense of accomplishment as you overcome each obstacle, reflecting on the sheer beauty that surrounds you. Pause and embrace the opportunity to absorb the tranquility and grandeur of the Shenandoah Valley stretched out beneath you.

At the summit of Bearfence Mountain, you'll be rewarded with an awe-inspiring 360-degree view. Take a moment to savor the panoramic splendor that unfolds before you. Gaze out at the seemingly endless waves of lush forest, the meandering rivers, and the distant ridges that define the landscape. It's an experience that leaves an indelible mark on your soul—a testament to nature's majestic artistry.

As you continue your journey, the trail presents more opportunities for rock scrambling, each one more thrilling than the last. Embrace the challenge, knowing that each climb brings with it the promise of ever more breathtaking vistas. Engage your senses fully, inhaling the fresh mountain air, feeling the texture of the rocks beneath your fingertips, and immersing yourself in the serenity of the natural world.

As you descend from Bearfence Mountain, take a moment to reflect on the extraordinary adventure you've just undertaken. The memories you've created and the challenges you've conquered will forever be etched in your heart. Remember, the ascent is only half of the journey; the descent offers its unique perspective, revealing hidden nooks and crannies of the mountain that may have gone unnoticed on the way up.

Once your Bearfence Mountain expedition is complete, reward yourself with a well-deserved rest. Return to the comforts of Shenandoah National Park and indulge in the amenities provided. Whether you choose to relax at one of the park's scenic picnic areas or retell your stories of triumph at a cozy lodge, take the time to relish the extraordinary accomplishment you've achieved.

Appalachian Trail

The Appalachian Trail, stretching over 2,000 miles from Georgia to Maine, traverses 101 magnificent miles through Shenandoah National Park. This area of the trail promises an immersive experience that will leave you breathless, both from the physical challenge it presents and the mesmerizing vistas that it unveils. Are you ready to follow in the footsteps of countless adventurers who have dared to take on this legendary trail?

As you set foot onto the Appalachian Trail within Shenandoah National Park, a sense of anticipation fills the air. This is your chance to immerse yourself in an epic adventure, forge a connection with nature, and push your boundaries. The trail beckons, weaving its way through ancient mountains and captivating forests, promising an experience like no other.

Prepare yourself for a trail that meanders through diverse landscapes, presenting you with a constantly changing tapestry of nature's wonders. As you hike, the trail will take you through dense forests, where sunlight dances through the leaves, casting gentle beams on the ground beneath your feet. Meandering streams will accompany your journey, their melodic murmurs providing a soothing soundtrack to your hike. It is a symphony of sights and sounds, designed to transport you to a place of serenity and rejuvenation.

The Appalachian Trail within Shenandoah National Park offers a range of challenges to satisfy every adventurer's appetite. From steep ascents that push your limits to rocky ridges that require nimble footwork, the trail presents myriad opportunities for growth and self-discovery. As you tackle each obstacle, be sure to pause and appreciate the journey. Take a moment to reflect on the fortitude it takes to conquer each challenge and marvel at the breathtaking beauty that surrounds you.

Along the trail, prepare to encounter an abundance of wildlife. Be on the lookout for deer, their graceful presence is a reminder of the harmony between the animal kingdom and the natural environment. Listen for the cheerful songs of birds echoing through the trees, and keep an eye out for the occasional glimpse of a black bear or a shy fox. These encounters offer a precious connection with the wildlife that calls Shenandoah National Park home.

The true essence of the Appalachian Trail lies not only in its physical challenges and majestic scenery but also in the rich history and vibrant community that inhabit its spaces. As you hike, keep in mind the countless stories that have unfolded along this trail. From Native American tribes who once roamed these lands to pioneers who blazed the trail centuries ago, the Appalachian Trail is steeped in a legacy that can be felt with each step. Embrace this spirit of camaraderie as you encounter fellow hikers, sharing tales of triumph and challenges overcome. The Appalachian Trail community is a tapestry of diverse backgrounds and experiences, united by a shared love for the trail and the transformative power it holds.

Throughout your journey, remember to always be prepared. The Appalachian Trail can be both magnificent and demanding, testing your physical endurance and stamina. Pack essential gear, including sturdy hiking boots, layers of clothing to accommodate changing weather conditions, and sufficient food and water to keep you energized. Consult reliable maps and guides to ensure you stay on the right path and familiarize yourself with the safety protocols and regulations set forth by Shenandoah National Park.

As your adventure on the Appalachian Trail within Shenandoah National Park comes to a close, take a moment to reflect on the magnitude of your achievement. The memories you've created, the challenges you've conquered, and the awe-inspiring moments you've witnessed will forever hold a special place in your heart. The Appalachian Trail is not just a trail; it's a transformative experience, a journey that leaves an indelible mark on your soul.

As we bid farewell to this incredible trail, know that the call of the Appalachian Trail will forever echo in your heart. Carry its spirit with you as you venture forth into new adventures and continue your exploration of the natural world. The Appalachian Trail is a testament to the resilience of the human spirit and the enduring allure of nature's wonders. Cherish the memories made, the lessons learned, and the connections forged along this remarkable trail.

Thus, it is important to note that this classification is based on the overall difficulty level of the trails, taking into account factors such as terrain, elevation changes, and trail length. Please note that the classification of moderate and challenging trails can vary based on individual hiking experience and fitness level. It's always important to assess your capabilities and prepare accordingly before attempting any hike. Whether you choose an easy, moderate, or challenging trail, each one offers its unique rewards and stunning natural beauty to be discovered. Enjoy your hiking adventures in Shenandoah National Park.

Chapter 5: Historical Exploration

Historical Sites

Embark on a captivating journey through time as you explore the rich tapestry of history woven into the fabric of Shenandoah National Park. Delve into the stories and legacies of the past as you discover the park's fascinating historical sites, each offering a glimpse into the region's vibrant heritage and cultural significance.

Rapidan Camp: President Hoover's Retreat

Rapidan Camp, affectionately known as "The First Family's Forest Camp," served as President Herbert Hoover's secluded sanctuary amidst the beauty of Shenandoah National Park. This charming retreat, situated along the banks of the Rapidan River, was established in the early 1920s and saw frequent visits by the president and his close associates.

As you explore Rapidan Camp, you'll encounter a cluster of 13 cabins, each with its unique character and purpose. The Brown House, as the central dwelling, served as the primary residence for the president and First Lady Lou Henry Hoover. Admire the rustic architecture and be transported back to a time when simplicity and tranquility were cherished.

The surrounding structures, including the Prime Minister's Cabin and the Fisherman's Cabin, hosted various dignitaries and guests who were fortunate enough to receive President Hoover's invitation. Imagine the important conversations and decisions that were made within these walls, shaping the destiny of a nation.

Take a stroll along the Camp Hoover Trail, winding through the peaceful forest, and immerse yourself in the natural beauty that captivated President Hoover. The tranquil ambiance, combined with the echoes of the past, will create a profound connection to the history of this remarkable retreat.

Big Meadows: A Witness to Civil War

Big Meadows, a vast expanse of meadowland nestled within the heart of Shenandoah National Park, bore witness to the struggles and sacrifices of the Civil War. During the tumultuous years of the conflict, this peaceful terrain became a staging area, encampments, and even a battlefield.

As you traverse the meadows, you may encounter remnants of Civil War-era trench lines and fortifications, reminding you of the hardships faced by soldiers on both sides of the conflict. The peaceful tranquility of Big Meadows today stands in stark contrast to the turmoil of the past.

Reflect upon the stories of valor and resilience as you envision the soldiers who once sought solace in this natural haven amidst the chaos of war. The whispers of history permeate the gentle breeze, inviting you to embark on a journey of remembrance and understanding.

Skyland Resort: Hospitality with a Historic Flavor

Perched at an elevation of over 3,600 feet, Skyland Resort has been a cherished destination within Shenandoah National Park since the early 20th century. The resort's historic charm and breathtaking vistas of the surrounding mountains make it an ideal base for those seeking both relaxation and exploration.

Originally a hiker's hostel, Skyland Resort gradually evolved into a beloved retreat for travelers from near and far. As you arrive at the resort, feel a sense of awe at its idyllic location and the panoramic views that stretch as far as the eye can see.

Indulge in the delectable cuisine served at the rustic dining facilities, which boast a menu inspired by both regional favorites and classic dishes. Whether you're savoring a hearty breakfast or a delightful dinner, the historic ambiance of Skyland Resort elevates the culinary experience.

Allow yourself to unwind, enveloped by the tranquility of the surroundings. Take a moment to sit on the veranda, drink in the beauty of the mountains, and reflect on the countless travelers who have passed through this historic refuge, finding solace in the embrace of nature.

Nicholson Cabin: A Glimpse of Early Settlers

Nestled in a serene corner of Shenandoah National Park, Nicholson Cabin stands as a testament to the perseverance and resilience of early settlers in the Shenandoah Valley. Step across the threshold of this well-preserved cabin, and you'll be transported to a time when self-sufficiency and survival were paramount.

As you explore the rooms within Nicholson Cabin, observe the humble yet ingenious craftsmanship that reflects the resourcefulness of those who crafted this abode. Traces of the past linger in every corner, from the creaking wooden floorboards to the simple furniture that provided comfort in this rugged environment.

Immerse yourself in the stories of the settlers who called this cabin home, imagining the challenges they faced as they carved out a living in the wilderness. Their toil and determination paved the way for the establishment of communities that eventually evolved into the vibrant towns we know today.

Allow the whispers of history to guide your journey, connecting you with the struggles and triumphs of those who called this secluded cabin their own.

South River Picnic Area: Relics of a Bygone Era

Hidden within the embrace of Shenandoah National Park lies the South River Picnic Area, a place where remnants of a once-thriving community are scattered amidst the tranquil beauty of nature. As you wander through this serene setting, observe the worn-down stone foundations and chimney stacks that bear witness to a bygone era.

In the past, the South River Picnic Area was home to a thriving community centered around amill and various other structures. The bustling activity of this community served as a vital hub for the local population, providing sustenance and a sense of community.

Today, nature has reclaimed the area, wrapping it in a cloak of peaceful serenity. The remnants of the past serve as a poignant reminder of the passage of time and the impermanence of human endeavors. It is a place of reflection and contemplation, where the echoes of the past merge with the soothing sounds of the flowing river, inviting you to pause and ponder the stories that have transpired here.

As you meander through the South River Picnic Area, let your imagination transport you to a time when laughter filled the air and the sound of bustling activity echoed through the valley. While the echoes may have faded, their essence can still be felt, connecting you with the lives that once thrived within this picturesque landscape.

Lewis Mountain Cabins: An African American Legacy

Tucked away amidst the mountains of Shenandoah National Park, Lewis Mountain Cabins bear witness to the resilience and sense of community that defined the African American experience during a time of segregation. These humble cabins provided a refuge and gathering place for African American families, who sought solace and connection amidst the tranquil beauty of the mountains.

As you step through the doors of Lewis Mountain Cabins, you'll be enveloped in the warmth and history that permeates each dwelling. These cabins hold within their walls the stories of triumph over adversity, of determination and spirit.

Imagine life as it once was for the African American families who sought respite within these cabins. Picture the laughter and joy that filled the air as families gathered to share meals, stories, and songs.

Sense the strength that was forged within these walls, as individuals navigated the challenges of a world that didn't always recognize their worth.

Lewis Mountain Cabins offers a window into the African American legacy within Shenandoah National Park, reminding us of the significant contributions and indomitable spirit of a community that persevered against the odds. Their stories, resonating with strength and resilience, add layers of depth and meaning to the fabric of the park's history.

Appalachian Trail Museum: Honoring an Iconic Journey

Situated near the entrance of Shenandoah National Park, the Appalachian Trail Museum stands as a tribute to the iconic trail and the trailblazers who dedicated their lives to its creation. Journey inside this engaging museum, and embark on a captivating exploration of the history, challenges, and triumphs associated with this renowned footpath.

The exhibits within the Appalachian Trail Museum offer a comprehensive understanding of the trail's origins, showcasing the vision and perseverance of those who conceptualized and built this extraordinary pathway. Discover the obstacles that were overcome, the natural wonders that await discovery, and the immeasurable impact the trail has had on both individuals and communities along its path.

Take a moment to imagine yourself donning a backpack and setting foot on this iconic journey, meandering through stunning landscapes and connecting with fellow hikers who share the same spirit of adventure. The Appalachian Trail Museum serves as a gateway to an unparalleled experience, inspiring awe and wanderlust within all who step through its doors.

Take the time to immerse yourself in the narratives woven within the walls of this museum, allowing them to kindle a flame of curiosity and appreciation for the trail's rich history. Whether you are a seasoned thru-hiker or simply an admirer of nature's wonders, the Appalachian Trail Museum offers a fascinating insight into the indomitable human spirit and the transformative power of wilderness exploration.

Stony Man Mountain: Standing Tall in History

Ascending to an elevation of 4,031 feet, Stony Man Mountain stands as a towering testament to both natural beauty and historical significance within Shenandoah National Park. This majestic peak, named after the legendary Northern Cherokee leader, offers panoramic vistas that stretch across the park and beyond.

Traverse the well-marked trails that wind their way up Stony Man Mountain, and imagine the stories of the indigenous peoples who once called this place home. Delve into the rich cultural heritage that lies within the embrace of these ancient mountains, connecting with their timeless spirit.

As you stand upon the summit, basking in the breathtaking views, reflect upon the impact of Stony Man Mountain on the history of this region. From notable explorers and early settlers to those who fought to preserve its natural splendor, the mountain has been at the heart of human endeavors for centuries.

Dark Hollow Falls: Cascading Beauty and Tales of the Past

Tucked away within the enchanting embrace of Shenandoah National Park, Dark Hollow Falls presents a captivating tapestry of cascading water and ancient geological formations. As you trek along the trail that leads to the falls, allow your senses to absorb the serenity and sheer beauty of the surroundings.

While Dark Hollow Falls is renowned for its natural splendor, it also holds stories of the past that whisper through the rustling leaves and glistening cascades. This secluded haven was once frequented by moonshiners during the Prohibition era, finding solace amidst the roaring waters and dense forests.

As you stand before the falls, envision the clandestine activities that took place in this very spot. Feel the thrill of the chase as law enforcement pursued those who sought to defy the restrictions of the time. Let the mist of the falls transport you back to an era of secrecy and rebellion, infusing in you tales of resilience and the pursuit of freedom.

Pinnacles Overlook: A Window to Geological Time

Perched atop the Blue Ridge Mountains, the Pinnacles Overlook offers a breathtaking vantage point where you can witness the dynamic forces that shaped Shenandoah National Park over millions of years. Gaze out at the serrated, rocky formations that command attention, their stark beauty reflecting the passage of time.

As you stand on this precipice, take a journey through the geologic history that lies beneath your feet. The layers of ancient sediments, sculpted by the relentless forces of wind and water, reveal the story of Earth's ever-changing landscapes. Let the majesty of the Pinnacles Overlook inspire your words to paint vivid scenes of primordial forces and the enduring essence of nature.

Allow the primal energy of this overlook to ignite your imagination as you craft narratives that explore the interplay of humans and their environment. The tales you weave can draw upon the resilience of the land and the triumphs of those who champion its conservation, preserving its beauty for generations to come.

Bearfence Mountain: A Playground of Rocks and Memories

Nestled in the heart of Shenandoah National Park, Bearfence Mountain promises an exhilarating adventure where nature's playground intertwines with tales of outdoor exploration. Known for its unique summit and thrilling rock scramble, this mountain invites visitors to test their mettle and forge lasting memories.

Embark on the Bearfence Mountain Loop Trail, relishing every step as you navigate through the boulder-strewn landscape. Channel the spirit of past adventurers who embraced the challenge of the rock scramble, their laughter, and exhilaration echoing through the misty forest.

As you reach the summit of Bearfence Mountain, drink in the sweeping views of the surrounding Shenandoah Valley, a testament to the beauty that lies within this rugged terrain. Capture the sense of adventure, freedom, and triumph that permeates the air, bringing your characters to life against the backdrop of this thrilling landscape.

Draw upon the memories etched into Bearfence Mountain, allowing them to infuse your storytelling with the universal themes of perseverance, fearlessness, and the transformative power of exploration.

Overall Run Falls: A Symphony of Water and Wilderness

Flowing gracefully through the lush landscapes of Shenandoah National Park, Overall Run Falls is the crown jewel of the park's cascading wonders. Plunging over 93 feet in a series of magnificent tiers, this majestic waterfall captivates the senses, leaving an indelible mark on all who encounter its beauty.

Hike along the trail that winds its way to Overall Run Falls, immersing yourself in the symphony of nature that accompanies your journey. The song of birds, the rustling of leaves, and the murmurs of the falls intertwine with one another, creating a harmonious melody that transports you to a realm untouched by time.

Marvel at the sheer power and elegance of Overall Run Falls as it cascades down the rocky cliffs, plunging into the pool below. The spray of mist caresses your skin, awakening your senses and igniting your creativity. Allow the tranquility of this hidden oasis to be your muse as you weave tales of self-discovery, resilience, and the profound connections we forge with nature.

As you explore these historical sites within Shenandoah National Park, be sure to immerse yourself fully in the stories they hold. Let their whispers guide your footsteps and ignite your imagination, as you connect with the diverse array of people, events, and legacies that have shaped this extraordinary park.

Native American History

In the midst of the breathtaking beauty of Shenandoah National Park lies a rich and diverse history deeply intertwined with the land itself. As you embark on your journey through the park, allow yourself to be immersed in the captivating stories of the Native American tribes that once thrived in this region. Discover the vibrant tapestry of their traditions, spirituality, and survival in the face of change. Let's delve into the fascinating history of the Native American tribes that once called Shenandoah National Park home.

The Powhatan Confederacy

The Powhatan Confederacy, led by Chief Powhatan, was comprised of Algonquian-speaking tribes who inhabited the fertile coastal plains of Virginia. These tribes, including the Pamunkey, Mattaponi, and Chickahominy, had a deep connection to the land and its abundant resources. They relied on hunting, fishing, and cultivating maize, beans, and squash to sustain their communities. Their settlements were characterized by longhouses, where extended families lived together, fostering a sense of unity and cooperation. Today, you can explore the remnants of their villages, gaining insights into their way of life and the skills they possess, such as intricate pottery and weaving techniques.

The Monacan Nation

The Monacan people, one of the oldest known tribes in Virginia, occupied the pristine Blue Ridge Mountains. They were skilled hunters, gatherers, and farmers, utilizing the resources of the mountains to meet their needs. With a deep reverence for the natural world, the Monacan people believed that everything possessed a spirit, and they sought to maintain harmony with their surroundings. Examine their ceremonial grounds, where they performed rituals to honor the mountains and connect with their ancestral spirits. Admire their artistry, displayed through intricate beadwork, basketry, and pottery, which encapsulate the unique beauty of their culture.

The Cherokee Nation

The Cherokee Nation, originating from the southeast region, made their presence known in the valleys of Shenandoah National Park. They were an agrarian tribe, cultivating crops such as corn, beans, and squash using innovative methods. The Cherokee held a deep spiritual connection to the land, attributing spiritual beings and animal guides to various natural features. Explore their ancient villages and ceremonial grounds, where you can gain insights into their agricultural practices and witness the stunning craftsmanship of their art, including woodcarvings, beadwork, and intricate woven blankets.

The Shawnee Nation

The Shawnee Nation, renowned for their hunting and fishing skills, thrived in the regions surrounding the Shenandoah River. They possessed an intimate knowledge of the land, relying on the river and its abundant resources for sustenance. The Shawnee people were also skilled traders, establishing extensive networks that allowed them to exchange goods and ideas with neighboring tribes. As you wander along the Shenandoah River, take a moment to reflect on the Shawnee's deep connection to this waterway and their reverence for the natural world that sustained them.

The Catawba Nation

The Catawba Nation, with its origins in the Southern Appalachian Highlands, demonstrated remarkable agricultural expertise. They constructed terraced fields, and ingeniously adapted to the mountainous terrain, to cultivate maize, beans, and other crops. The Catawba people also excelled in crafting pottery and baskets, showcasing their artistic skills and creativity. As you wander through the southern regions of Shenandoah National Park, you can still witness the remnants of their agricultural terraces, a testament to their intimate bond with the land and their determination to thrive in challenging environments.

Immerse yourself in the captivating history of these Native American tribes as you explore Shenandoah National Park. Their existence and contributions, deeply entwined with the land, serve as a reminder of the enduring legacy they have left behind.

Events and Festivals

Shenandoah National Park isn't just about breathtaking vistas and challenging hikes. It's a living tapestry woven with stories of human history, diverse ecosystems, and vibrant cultural traditions. Immerse yourself in this tapestry by attending one of the many cultural events and festivals held throughout the year in the park and surrounding communities.

Within the Park

- April 20th: Fee-Free Day: Celebrate National Park Week with free entry to Shenandoah National Park!
- April 27th: Junior Ranger Day: Engage your children in interactive activities and earn a Junior Ranger badge at various visitor centers.
- May 11th: Youth Art Contest Winner Ceremony: Witness the artistic talents of young minds at the Byrd Visitor Center.
- May 11th-12th: Wildflower Weekend: Immerse yourself in the vibrant colors and delicate aromas of blooming wildflowers during guided hikes and educational programs.
- June: Shenandoah Valley Artfest: Immerse yourself in the creative spirit of the region at this one-day celebration of art, music, and

culture in downtown Woodstock, close to the park's northern entrance.

- July 4th: Independence Day Celebration: Celebrate America's birthday with ranger-led programs, live music, and fireworks displays at Skyland Lodge.
- August 2nd-4th: Night Sky Festival: Gaze at the stars with expert rangers, participate in astronomy workshops, and experience the magic of the night sky amidst the mountains.
- August 4th: Fee-Free Day: Celebrate the National Park Service birthday with free entry to Shenandoah National Park!
- September 7th-8th: Wilderness Weekend: Embark on guided hikes, learn about wilderness stewardship, and connect with the wild side of the park.
- September 28th: Fee-Free Day: Celebrate National Public Lands Day with free entry to Shenandoah National Park!
- October: Fall Foliage Festival: Witness the breathtaking transformation of the park into a fiery canvas of reds, oranges, and yellows through scenic drives, ranger-led hikes, and special programs.
- December: Holiday Lantern Walk: Celebrate the season with a magical walk through luminary displays at Skyland Lodge.

Surrounding Communities

Luray

- January: Winterfest in Luray Caverns (various dates): Explore the caverns adorned with dazzling holiday lights.
- May: Luray Spring Wine Festival (various dates): Sample exquisite wines from Virginia wineries and enjoy live music.
- October: Luray Car & Craft Festival (various dates): Immerse yourself in classic cars, handcrafted goods, and live music.
- December: Luray Main Street Christmas Parade & Celebration (early December): Enjoy a festive parade, holiday shopping, and festive activities.

Front Royal

- April: Annual Shenandoah Apple Blossom Festival (various dates): Celebrate Spring with parades, live music, crafts, and, of course, apple pie!
- July: Royal Fireworks Celebration (4th July): Enjoy spectacular fireworks display and family-friendly festivities.
- August: Front Royal Blues Festival (various dates): Immerse yourself in the soulful sounds of blues music.
- October: Civil War Weekend at Cedar Hill (various dates): Step back in time with living history demonstrations, battle reenactments, and educational programs.

Massanutten Resort

- Year-round: Various festivals and events, including Oktoberfest, Winterfest, and Food & Wine Festival. Consult the resort website for specific dates.

Harrisonburg

- March: Virginia Film Festival (various dates): Celebrate independent and international cinema.
- May: Shenandoah Shakespeare Festival (various dates): Enjoy live performances of Shakespearean plays outdoors.
- October: Harrisonburg Wine & Harvest Festival (various dates): Sample local wines, savor delicious food, and enjoy live music.
- December: Christkindlmarkt (various dates): Experience the charm of a traditional German Christmas market.
- Remember: Dates and schedules may vary. Always check the official websites or contact event organizers for the latest information before planning your trip.

Additional Tips

- Plan ahead: Popular events can fill up quickly, so book accommodations and purchase tickets in advance when necessary.

- Embrace the crowds: Be prepared for larger crowds during major events, and practice patience and courtesy.
- Respect the environment: Minimize your impact by following responsible practices like waste disposal and staying on designated trails.

By attending cultural events and festivals, you can gain a deeper appreciation for the history, traditions, and vibrant spirit of the Shenandoah region. Let your visit go beyond

Art and Craft Exhibits

Beyond the breathtaking vistas and challenging hikes, Shenandoah National Park pulsates with the creative spirit of the region. Immerse yourself in this vibrant tapestry by exploring the stunning art and craft exhibits within the park and surrounding communities.

Within the Park

Skyland Lodge Art Gallery: Let art and nature intertwine as you browse rotating exhibits showcasing regional artists inspired by Shenandoah's majestic landscapes. Engage with artists during talks and workshops, gaining insights into their creative processes and the stories woven into their works.

Big Meadows Wayside Exhibit: Journey back in time through historic photographs and artifacts that tell the tale of the Civilian Conservation Corps and their enduring artistic contributions to the park. Gain an appreciation for the rustic cabins, stonework, and scenic overlooks that remain a testament to their artistry.

Sky Meadows Arts Center: Nestled near the park's northern entrance, this haven for creativity hosts workshops, art shows, and lectures throughout the year. Immerse yourself in diverse artistic expressions, from traditional crafts to contemporary paintings, and discover hidden talents among local artists.

Venture Beyond the Park

Luray

Luray Caverns Gift Shop: Delve into the subterranean wonders of Luray Caverns and then ascend to the surface to discover locally crafted treasures. Adorn yourself with jewelry inspired by sparkling stalactites, browse pottery reminiscent of the caverns' organic forms, and take home a unique piece imbued with the magic of the underworld.

Luray Main Street: During the summer months, the picturesque Main Street transforms into an open-air gallery. Stroll amidst vibrant displays by local artists, each showcasing their unique styles and mediums. Converse with the creators, learn about their inspirations, and perhaps find the perfect souvenir that encapsulates the town's artistic spirit.

Front Royal

Artworks Gallery: Embark on a visual journey through the diverse talents of regional artists at Artworks Gallery in downtown Front Royal. Explore a spectrum of styles and mediums, from captivating landscapes to abstract sculptures, and discover hidden gems waiting to be appreciated.

The Artful Dodger: Immerse yourself in the collaborative spirit of this cooperative gallery showcasing works by over 30 local artists. Wander through a treasure trove of paintings, sculptures, and crafts, each imbued with the individual flair and personality of its creator. Converse with the artists, delve into their creative narratives, and find a one-of-a-kind piece to cherish.

Massanutten Resort

Art in the Heart Festival (June): Immerse yourself in a vibrant weekend celebration of art at Massanutten Resort. Witness live demonstrations by skilled artisans, explore diverse exhibition booths brimming with creativity and engage with the artistic community. Let the infectious energy of this festival ignite your artistic spirit.

Harrisonburg

Artful Friday (Second Friday of every month): On the second Friday of each month, Harrisonburg comes alive with artistic energy. Galleries, studios, and museums open their doors late, offering special events, refreshments, and the opportunity to connect with the local art scene. Explore diverse exhibitions, engage with artists, and experience the vibrant pulse of Harrisonburg's creative community.

James Madison University Galleries: Delve into the world of established and emerging artists at the James Madison University Galleries. Immerse yourself in thought-provoking exhibitions spanning various mediums, genres, and artistic movements. Be inspired by the innovative spirit of these galleries and discover new perspectives on the world around you.

Shenandoah Valley Art Center: Journey through the ever-evolving landscape of contemporary art at the Shenandoah Valley Art Center. Explore captivating exhibitions, participate in educational programs and workshops, and be a part of the vibrant dialogue surrounding art in the region. Let the center ignite your curiosity, challenge your perceptions, and leave you with a deeper appreciation for the power of artistic expression.

Embrace the Creative Journey

Your exploration of art and craft exhibits in Shenandoah and beyond is not just about acquiring souvenirs; it's about connecting with the soul of the region. Engage with artists, delve into their stories, and appreciate the craftsmanship behind each piece. Support local communities by purchasing their creations, ensuring the artistic legacy continues to thrive. Remember, every artwork holds a unique narrative, waiting to be discovered and cherished. So, embark on your creative journey, explore the hidden gems, and allow the artistic spirit of Shenandoah to enrich your experience.

Chapter 6: Top Attractions

Skyline Drive

Skyline Drive, stretching 105 miles along the crest of the Blue Ridge Mountains in Shenandoah National Park, offers one of the most scenic drives in the United States. This iconic roadway runs from Front Royal in the north to Rockfish Gap in the south, providing breathtaking views of the Shenandoah Valley to the west and the Piedmont region to the east. As you drive along Skyline Drive, you are treated to panoramic vistas, lush forests, and abundant wildlife. The road is lined with 75 overlooks, each offering a unique perspective of the park's stunning landscapes. Skyline Drive is open year-round, weather permitting, and is the only public road through the park, making it an essential part of any visit to Shenandoah National Park.

History of Skyline Drive

Early Beginnings

The concept of Skyline Drive was first proposed in the early 1920s as part of the effort to establish a national park in the eastern United States. The Southern Appalachian National Park Committee, tasked with finding a suitable location, identified the Blue Ridge Mountains of Virginia as an ideal site due to its proximity to major eastern cities and its natural beauty. In 1924, William C. Gregg, a member of the committee, suggested the idea of a "ridge road" that would follow the mountaintop, offering continuous views of the Shenandoah Valley and the Piedmont Plain.

Construction and Development

Construction of Skyline Drive began in 1931, even before Shenandoah National Park was officially established. The project was part of a broader initiative to provide employment during the Great Depression, utilizing funds from emergency employment relief programs. The Civilian Conservation Corps (CCC), established by President Franklin D. Roosevelt, played a crucial role in the construction of the drive. The CCC "boys" did not build the roadbed itself but were responsible for grading the slopes, constructing overlooks, guardrails, and stone walls, and landscaping the areas alongside the road. They also built picnic areas, campgrounds, visitor centers, and maintenance buildings, contributing significantly to the infrastructure and visitor amenities of the park.

Opening and Early Years

Skyline Drive officially opened to the public on October 1, 1934, even though the park was not formally established until 1935. The drive quickly became popular due to its accessibility and the spectacular views it offered. The initial section from Thornton Gap to Swift Run Gap, covering 32 miles, was the first to open. By 1939, the entire 105-mile length of Skyline Drive was completed, providing a continuous scenic route through the park.

Post-War Enhancements

After World War II, the National Park Service undertook several projects to enhance Skyline Drive. This included rebuilding many of the original chestnut log guardrails, which had rotted and were removed in the 1950s. The CCC's work was further reinforced with modern construction techniques, ensuring the longevity and safety of the structures along the drive.

Key Features of Shenandoah National Park

Skyline Drive

Skyline Drive is the park's most famous feature, running 105 miles along the crest of the Blue Ridge Mountains. This scenic roadway offers 75 overlooks where you can stop to enjoy panoramic views of the Shenandoah Valley to the west and the Piedmont region to the east. It is open year-round, weather permitting, and provides access to numerous trails and park facilities.

Hiking Trails

The park boasts over 500 miles of hiking trails, including a 101-mile segment of the Appalachian Trail. Popular hikes include Old Rag Mountain, known for its challenging rock scrambles and stunning summit views, and Dark Hollow Falls, an accessible trail leading to one of the park's most beautiful waterfalls. Trails range from easy walks to strenuous climbs, catering to all levels of hikers.

Wildlife

Shenandoah National Park is home to a diverse array of wildlife. Visitors can expect to see white-tailed deer, black bears, wild turkeys, and more than 200 bird species. The park's biodiversity makes it a prime location for wildlife watching and birding throughout the year.

Historical Sites

The park preserves several historical sites, including Rapidan Camp, the summer retreat of President Herbert Hoover. This historic site offers guided tours that provide insight into its significance during Hoover's presidency. Additionally, remnants of old homesteads and family cemeteries scattered throughout the park tell the stories of the mountain communities displaced to create the park.

Visitor Centers

Dickey Ridge Visitor Center and Harry F. Byrd, Sr. Visitor Center are key facilities offering educational exhibits, park information, and ranger-led programs. These centers help visitors plan their trips, learn about the park's natural and cultural history, and access essential services.

Best Times to Visit and What to Expect

- Best Time to Visit: Spring and fall are ideal times for a drive along Skyline Drive. Spring offers blooming wildflowers and mild temperatures, while fall provides breathtaking foliage.
- What to Expect: Skyline Drive stretches 105 miles along the crest of the Blue Ridge Mountains, providing stunning panoramic views. This scenic byway features over 75 overlooks, each offering unique vistas of the Shenandoah Valley and Piedmont. As you drive, you will encounter mileposts that guide you to notable stops and attractions.

Notable Stops

- Dickey Ridge Visitor Center (Mile 4.6): A perfect starting point for your journey, offering exhibits, maps, and ranger-guided information.
- Range View Overlook (Mile 17.1): Provides a sweeping view of the rolling Blue Ridge Mountains.
- Big Meadows (Mile 51): Known for its open fields and frequent wildlife sightings, especially white-tailed deer.
- Hogback Overlook (Mile 20.7): Offers the longest and broadest panorama of any overlook along the drive.

Hiking Trails

- Best Time to Visit: Early summer and fall. Early summer offers lush greenery and pleasant weather, while fall provides cooler temperatures and beautiful autumn colors.
- What to Expect: Shenandoah boasts over 500 miles of trails, including a significant portion of the Appalachian Trail. These trails range from easy walks to challenging hikes, each providing unique views and experiences.

Notable Hikes

- Old Rag Mountain: One of the most popular and challenging hikes, featuring rock scrambles and stunning summit views. It's a strenuous 9.4-mile round-trip.
- Mary's Rock: Offers two routes to the summit with panoramic views of the Shenandoah Valley. The shorter trail is 2.6 miles round-trip, while the longer trail is 3.6 miles.
- Dark Hollow Falls: A shorter hike that leads to one of the park's most popular waterfalls. It's a 1.4-mile round-trip, making it accessible for most visitors.
- Rose River Falls: A moderately challenging 3.8-mile loop that showcases several beautiful waterfalls along the Rose River.

Historical and Cultural Significance

Best Time to Visit: Year-round, though spring and fall provide the best weather for exploring outdoor historical sites.

What to Expect: Shenandoah National Park is rich in history, from its early settlers to its establishment as a national park. Significant historical sites and stories add depth to your visit.

Notable Historical Sites

- Rapidan Camp: The summer retreat of President Herbert Hoover, offering guided tours that provide insight into presidential history and the park's past.
- Byrd Visitor Center: Located at Big Meadows, this center offers exhibits on the history and creation of the park, including the efforts of the Civilian Conservation Corps (CCC).

Waterfalls

Best Time to Visit: Spring and early summer, when the water flow is at its peak due to melting snow and seasonal rains.

What to Expect: Shenandoah is home to numerous waterfalls, each accessible by various hiking trails. These natural features provide serene spots for reflection and photography.

Notable Waterfalls

- Dark Hollow Falls: Easily accessible and one of the most visited waterfalls in the park.
- Doyles River Falls: A 3.4-mile round-trip hike that leads to two beautiful waterfalls, offering a more secluded experience.
- Rose River Falls: Accessible via a 3.8-mile loop trail, showcasing multiple cascades along the Rose River.

Wildlife Viewing

Best Time to Visit: Early morning or late afternoon, particularly in spring and fall when wildlife is most active.

What to Expect: Shenandoah's diverse habitats support a variety of wildlife. Visitors can expect to see white-tailed deer, black bears, wild turkeys, and over 200 species of birds.

Best Spots for Wildlife Viewing

- Big Meadows: A prime location for spotting white-tailed deer and other wildlife.
- Skyline Drive Overlooks: Various overlooks provide opportunities to observe wildlife in their natural habitats.

Visitor Centers

Best Time to Visit: Any time the park is open, with spring and fall offering the most comfortable weather for exploring exhibits and attending ranger programs.

What to Expect: Shenandoah's visitor centers are excellent starting points for your adventure, providing essential information, exhibits, and ranger-led programs.

Notable Visitor Centers

- Dickey Ridge Visitor Center (Mile 4.6): Offers panoramic views, exhibits, and ranger-led programs.
- Harry F. Byrd Visitor Center (Mile 51): Located in Big Meadows, this center provides comprehensive exhibits on the park's natural and cultural history.

Practical Tips

- Plan Your Stops: With 75 overlooks, it's easy to spend an entire day exploring. Planning your stops in advance can help you make the most of your time.
- Stay Informed: Check for road closures and weather conditions before you go. Inclement weather can cause sections of Skyline Drive to close temporarily.
- Fuel Up: Gas stations are scarce along Skyline Drive, so ensure your tank is full before entering the park.
- Respect Wildlife: Maintain a safe distance from animals and never feed them. Use pull-offs to safely observe wildlife without blocking traffic.

By visiting these top attractions and planning your trip during the optimal times, you can fully experience the beauty, history, and recreational opportunities that Shenandoah National Park has to offer.

Waterfalls

Shenandoah National Park is home to some of the most picturesque waterfalls in the eastern United States. Each waterfall offers a unique combination of scenic beauty, hiking adventure, and a connection to the natural world that leaves a lasting impression on visitors. Here are some of the most popular waterfalls in the park:

Dark Hollow Falls

Located near milepost 50.7 on Skyline Drive, Dark Hollow Falls is the park's most accessible and popular waterfall. This 70-foot waterfall is only a 1.4-mile round-trip hike from the parking area. The trail is moderately challenging, with a steep descent to the falls and a demanding climb back up. Despite the effort, the view of the cascading waters makes it a must-see. Note that pets are not allowed on this trail.

Rose River Falls

Rose River Falls, located at milepost 49.4, is a 67-foot waterfall that rewards hikers with stunning cascades, especially after rainfall. The 2.6-mile round-trip hike is moderately difficult, featuring an elevation gain of 720 feet. The trail is pet-friendly, allowing you to enjoy the hike with your furry companions. The serene environment and beautiful cascades make it a popular spot for both hiking and photography.

Overall Run Falls

As the tallest waterfall in Shenandoah National Park, Overall Run Falls stands at an impressive 93 feet. Located near milepost 21.1, the hike to the falls is a 6.5-mile round-trip that is considered moderately strenuous, with an elevation gain of 1,850 feet. This trail is also pet-friendly. The best time to visit is before June when the water flow is at its peak, ensuring a more dramatic view.

Doyles River Falls

Doyles River Falls, located at milepost 81.1, features two main cascades: the upper falls at 28 feet and the lower falls at 63 feet. The hike ranges from 2.7 miles to 7.8 miles round-trip, depending on the chosen route, with elevation gains from 850 to 1,825 feet. This moderately challenging hike provides multiple viewpoints and the option to extend the adventure to include Jones Run Falls via the Browns Gap Waterfall loop. The trails are pet-friendly, making them suitable for all visitors.

Jones Run Falls

Situated near milepost 84.1, Jones Run Falls is a 42-foot waterfall accessible via a 3.6-mile round-trip hike. The trail features a climb of 915 feet and can be extended to include Doyles River Falls. This moderate hike is known for its lush vegetation and tranquil setting, offering a peaceful retreat into nature. Pets are welcome on this trail, allowing you to bring your pet along for the adventure.

Lewis Falls

At milepost 51.4, Lewis Falls offers an 81-foot drop that can be viewed from a side trail. The 2.5-mile round-trip hike has an elevation gain of 795 feet and is considered moderately difficult due to its rocky and steep sections. It is recommended to visit early in the season or after rainfall for the best views. This trail is also pet-friendly.

South River Falls

Located at milepost 62.8, South River Falls boasts an 83-foot drop, making it the third tallest waterfall in the park. The 3.3-mile loop hike provides an overlook above the falls with an 850-foot elevation gain. This moderately challenging hike is ideal for those looking to experience the powerful flow of water and enjoy scenic views from the top. Pets are allowed on this trail, adding to its appeal.

Each of these waterfalls offers a unique experience, from easy strolls to more strenuous hikes, all providing a glimpse into the natural beauty and diverse ecosystems of Shenandoah National Park.

Chapter 7: Family-Friendly Activities

Junior Ranger Program

Exploring Shenandoah National Park with your family is a wonderful opportunity to create lasting memories and foster a love for the great outdoors. The park offers a variety of engaging activities specifically designed to entertain and educate young adventurers. Dive into the world of the Junior Ranger Program, a series of interactive experiences that will ignite the curiosity and enthusiasm of your little ones.

Junior Ranger Activity Book

The Junior Ranger Activity Book is carefully crafted to engage children in a wide range of activities designed to educate and entertain. As your child completes the various puzzles, quizzes, and challenges in the booklet, they will gain a deeper understanding of the park's ecosystems, geology, wildlife, and history. The activities are thoughtfully curated to be both enjoyable and educational, ensuring that young adventurers have a rewarding experience as they work towards earning their Junior Ranger badge.

Junior Ranger Discovery Kit

The Junior Ranger Discovery Kit is a treasure trove of exploration tools that empowers children to become independent learners and explorers. Inside the kit's backpack, your child will find essential equipment such as binoculars, field guides, magnifying lenses, and activity booklets. Armed with these resources, they can embark on their self-guided adventures through the park, observing and identifying the diverse flora and fauna, studying the geological features, and immersing themselves in the wonders of nature. The

Junior Ranger Discovery Kit encourages young minds to engage with the park's natural beauty on a deeper level.

Junior Ranger Wildlife Watchers

The Junior Ranger Wildlife Watchers program is perfect for young nature enthusiasts eager to discover the many inhabitants of Shenandoah National Park. Participants receive a comprehensive Wildlife Watchers booklet that serves as a field guide to the park's diverse wildlife. Using this guide, children can learn to identify various species of birds, mammals, reptiles, and amphibians, and gain knowledge about their behaviors and habitats. Whether they're spotting bobcats, listening for the melodies of songbirds, or observing elusive woodland creatures, the Wildlife Watchers program cultivates a sense of wonder and respect for the region's biodiversity.

Junior Ranger Archaeology Explorer

The Junior Ranger Archaeology Explorer program invites children to uncover the rich cultural history of Shenandoah National Park. By participating in this program, young adventurers will have the opportunity to delve into the stories and artifacts left behind by past civilizations. From examining historical objects to discovering archaeological sites, children will gain insights into the lives and traditions of those who once called this area home. The Archaeology Explorer program fosters an appreciation for the importance of preserving these archaeological treasures for future generations while igniting a passion for history and cultural heritage.

Junior Ranger Night Explorer

The Junior Ranger Night Explorer program unlocks the mysteries of the universe and provides a chance for children to explore the wonders of the night sky. Participants receive a Night Explorer booklet that introduces them to the fascinating realms of astronomy. With the guidance of this booklet, your child will learn about constellations, planets, and celestial events visible in Shenandoah National Park's clear night sky. Through stargazing, learning about the phases of the moon, and discovering fascinating astronomical phenomena, young explorers will develop an enduring fascination for the universe and its infinite wonders.

Thus, by participating in these Junior Ranger Programs, children will enhance their understanding of Shenandoah National Park, develop valuable insights into its natural and cultural heritage, and cultivate a deep appreciation for conservation and stewardship. These engaging and educational programs are carefully designed to spark a lifelong love for nature and foster a sense of adventure and responsibility in young minds. So, embrace the opportunities offered by these programs, and let your child's journey in Shenandoah National Park be filled with endless exploration and discovery.

Picnicking Areas and Family-Friendly Trails

Picnicking Areas

Big Meadows Picnic Area

Discover the tranquil beauty of the Big Meadows Picnic Area, located in the heart of Shenandoah National Park. This idyllic spot beckons you to indulge in a delightful picnic while surrounded by sweeping panoramic views. The open meadows provide a sense of serenity, inviting you to relax and enjoy the company of your loved ones amidst nature's splendor. With a plentiful supply of picnic tables and grills, your picnic experience is guaranteed to be comfortable and convenient.

Location

You can find the Big Meadows Picnic Area within Shenandoah National Park, near the Big Meadows Campground. Conveniently accessible from Skyline Drive, the park's main thoroughfare, it is easy to reach and well-marked.

How to Get There

To reach the Big Meadows Picnic Area, simply take Skyline Drive to Milepost 51.2. Look for the signs indicating the picnic area and follow the road that leads to the parking lot. From there, a short walk will take you to the picnic tables and grilling areas, ready to host your family gathering.

Dickey Ridge Picnic Area

Located near the northern entrance of Shenandoah National Park, the Dickey Ridge Picnic Area offers a serene and inviting atmosphere for families to unwind. Surrounded by lush greenery, this picturesque spot provides an escape from the hustle and bustle of everyday life. Plentiful picnic tables and grills are available, ensuring a comfortable and enjoyable picnic experience for you and your loved ones.

Location

The Dickey Ridge Picnic Area is situated near the Dickey Ridge Visitor Center, just off Skyline Drive. Its proximity to the park's entrance makes it easily accessible for visitors coming from the northern side.

How to Get There

To access the Dickey Ridge Picnic Area, follow Skyline Drive until you see the signs indicating the Dickey Ridge Visitor Center. The picnic area is located adjacent to the visitor center, making it convenient to park your vehicle and access the picnic tables and grilling areas.

Pinnacles Picnic Area

Explore the breathtaking beauty of the Pinnacles Picnic Area, nestled near the southern entrance of Shenandoah National Park. This peaceful and picturesque setting serves as a haven for families seeking solace amidst nature's grandeur. Surrounded by verdant forests and awe-inspiring vistas, this charming spot invites you to unwind and revel in quality time with your loved ones. Abundant picnic tables and grills ensure a comfortable and convenient picnic experience.

Location

The Pinnacles Picnic Area is located near the Swift Run Gap entrance of Shenandoah National Park, making it easily accessible for visitors entering the park from the southern side.

How to Get There

To reach the Pinnacles Picnic Area, follow Skyline Drive until you see the signs indicating the picnic area. Proceed along the well-marked road that leads to the parking lot. From there, a short walk will take you to the picnic tables and grilling areas, where you can enjoy a delightful family picnic surrounded by nature's splendor.

Family-Friendly Trails

Limberlost Trail

Embark on a family-friendly adventure along the Limberlost Trail, an accessible path near the Swift Run Gap entrance of Shenandoah National Park. This captivating trail spans 1.3 miles and meanders through beautiful forests and a charming wetland area. Its flat and well-maintained terrain makes it an ideal choice for families with younger children. Along the trail, informative signs offer glimpses into the park's diverse flora and fauna, enhancing your overall experience. Take your time exploring this enchanting trail and consider having a picnic at one of the designated spots along the route.

Location

You can access the Limberlost Trail near the Skyland area of Shenandoah National Park. Clear signage will guide you to the trailhead, and a parking area is available nearby.

How to Get There

From Skyline Drive, keep an eye out for signs directing you to the Limberlost Trail. Follow the designated road that leads you to the trailhead parking area. From there, accessing the trail and immersing yourself in its natural wonders couldn't be simpler.

Stony Man Trail

For families seeking a slightly more exhilarating yet rewarding experience, the Stony Man Trail is an excellent choice. This moderately challenging 1.6-mile trail offers captivating views and an opportunity to witness the park's iconic peak, Stony Man. As you traverse the well-maintained path, you'll encounter stunning rock formations, vibrant wildflowers, and panoramic vistas of the Shenandoah Valley. This family-friendly trail presents a perfect balance between adventure and accessibility, making it suitable for visitors of all ages.

Location

The Stony Man Trail can be accessed near the Skyland area of Shenandoah National Park. Its convenient location allows for easy exploration, especially for families staying in the nearby lodging facilities.

How to Get There

Follow the signs on Skyline Drive leading to Skyland. Once you've reached Skyland, look for directions to the Stony Man Trail. Parking is available nearby, and the trailhead is clearly marked. Lace up your hiking boots, gather your loved ones, and embark on an unforgettable journey.

Appalachian Trail

For those seeking a truly memorable family adventure, the Appalachian Trail offers boundless opportunities for exploration within Shenandoah National Park. This iconic trail spans over 100 miles through the park and offers various access points to cater to the preferences of different hikers. Along this renowned trail, families can admire stunning vistas, encounter unique wildlife, and immerse themselves in the tranquility of nature. Whether you choose to embark on a short section hike or a multi-day excursion, the Appalachian Trail promises an unforgettable experience for the entire family.

Location

The Appalachian Trail runs through Shenandoah National Park, offering numerous entry points along Skyline Drive. Consult the park maps or visitor center resources to determine the most suitable access point based on your desired hike length and difficulty level.

How to Get There

As you traverse Skyline Drive, keep an eye out for signs indicating the Appalachian Trail's entry points. These access points may require a short drive from Skyline Drive to their respective trailheads.

Safety Tips for Family Picnics

When picnicking in Shenandoah National Park, it is important to respect the park's rules and regulations to ensure the safety and preservation of the natural environment. Here are some specific guidelines that visitors should be aware of:

- Leave No Trace: Practice "Leave No Trace" principles by cleaning up after your picnic. Take all trash with you and dispose of it properly in designated receptacles outside the park. Leave the picnic area as pristine as you found it, so that others can enjoy its beauty too.
- Open Flames: Only use the designated grills provided in the picnic areas for cooking. Open fires and portable charcoal grills are not allowed due to the risk of wildfires. Follow all fire safety guidelines and ensure that fires are fully extinguished before leaving the area.

- Wildlife Interaction: Do not feed wildlife during your picnic. Feeding wildlife can disrupt their natural behavior and cause dependence on human food, which can have negative consequences for both animals and visitors. Observe wildlife from a safe distance and never attempt to approach or touch them.
- Respect Other Visitors: Keep noise levels to a minimum to avoid disturbing other picnickers and wildlife. Be mindful of others' space and privacy while enjoying your picnic. Additionally, avoid playing loud music, as it can disrupt the peaceful ambiance of the surroundings.
- Alcohol Consumption: While alcohol is permitted in picnic areas, it is important to consume it responsibly and be aware of the park's regulations regarding alcohol. Excessive alcohol consumption can impair judgment and pose safety risks, so it is advised to drink responsibly and be considerate of other park visitors.
- Permitted Hours: Picnic areas within Shenandoah National Park have specific operating hours. Ensure that you plan your picnic within these designated hours and be aware of any closures or restrictions that may be in place during certain times.
- Group Sizes: If you are planning a larger gathering or a group picnic, be mindful of specific regulations regarding group sizes. Some picnic areas may have restrictions to maintain the tranquility of the park and prevent overcrowding. Familiarize yourself with the capacity limits in each designated area to ensure compliance.
- Water Sources: While the park offers drinking water at various locations, not all picnic areas have immediate access to water sources. It's advisable to carry an ample supply of drinking water to stay hydrated throughout your picnic. Remember, leaving the picnic area to access water may disrupt the flow of your gathering or hike, so plan accordingly.
- Food Storage: To prevent interactions with wildlife and maintain cleanliness, it is crucial to store food securely. Consider using sealable containers or coolers that can be tightly closed and properly stored in designated areas or lockers. This will help

prevent curiosity from wildlife and reduce the risk of attracting them to picnic areas.

- Pet Regulations: Shenandoah National Park allows pets in designated picnic areas and campgrounds. However, they must be on a leash no longer than six feet and under control at all times. Properly clean up after pets to maintain the cleanliness and hygiene of picnic areas. Remember to respect other visitors' comfort and leash your pet if necessary.
- Trail Etiquette: If you decide to enjoy a picnic along one of the family-friendly trails mentioned earlier, it's important to follow trail etiquette. Yield to other hikers while being aware of your surroundings. Remember to stay on designated trails to protect fragile ecosystems and respect any trail restrictions or closures for safety purposes.
- Use of Disposable Items: When packing for your picnic, try to minimize the use of disposable items such as paper plates, plastic cutlery, and single-use plastic bottles. Opt for reusable materials whenever possible to reduce waste and minimize the impact on the environment. Consider bringing reusable containers, utensils, and water bottles to enjoy a more eco-friendly picnic experience.
- Accessibility: Shenandoah National Park makes every effort to provide accessible facilities and picnic areas for visitors with disabilities. Some picnic areas are equipped with accessible tables, restrooms, and parking spaces to ensure that everyone can enjoy the park's beauty. Check with park authorities or visit the official park website for specific information on accessible picnic areas.
- Fishing and Hunting Restrictions: While picnicking, it's important to note that fishing and hunting are regulated activities in Shenandoah National Park. Ensure that you are familiar with the specific rules and regulations regarding these activities, as well as any limitations on fishing spots or hunting areas within the park. Respect any restricted zones to maintain a safe and peaceful picnic environment.
- Trail Cleanliness: If you choose to enjoy a picnic along one of the park's scenic trails, it is crucial to maintain cleanliness and

minimize your impact on the surroundings. Pack out all garbage, including food scraps and wrappers, to preserve the natural beauty of the trails. Avoid littering and dispose of waste responsibly in designated trash receptacles outside the park.

- Weather Awareness: Keep an eye on the weather forecast before heading out for your picnic. Weather conditions in Shenandoah National Park can change rapidly, and it's important to be prepared for inclement weather. Carry appropriate gear such as rain jackets, sunscreen, insect repellent, and extra layers to ensure your comfort and safety during your picnic.

By familiarizing yourself with and adhering to these rules and regulations, you can contribute to the responsible enjoyment of Shenandoah National Park's picnic areas. These guidelines aim to ensure the safety and preservation of the park's natural beauty while allowing visitors to have a remarkable and enjoyable picnic experience with their families and friends.

Educational Opportunities for Kids

As a parent, exploring Shenandoah National Park with your family, you'll be delighted to discover the numerous educational opportunities available for children in the park. These experiences will not only entertain your little ones but also foster a deeper understanding and appreciation for the natural world. Here are some educational activities that will captivate and engage your children during your visit to Shenandoah National Park:

Junior Ranger Program: Engage your child's curiosity and facilitate their learning through the Junior Ranger program. Designed for children between the ages of 5 and 13, this program encourages young adventurers to complete a series of age-appropriate activities and earn a Junior Ranger badge. Stop by any visitor center to pick up a Junior Ranger booklet, which includes scavenger hunts, nature quizzes, and fun challenges that explore the park's flora, fauna, and cultural history.

Ranger-Led Discovery Programs: Shenandoah National Park offers a variety of ranger-led programs tailored to children. From guided hikes to interactive presentations, these programs provide hands-on learning experiences that immerse children in the park's natural wonders.

Embark on a guided nature walk where rangers introduce kids to the secrets of the forest, teaching them about various plants, animals, and geological features along the way. Be sure to check the park's event calendar for specific programs and their schedules.

Junior Wildflower Club: Does your child have a budding interest in botany? The Junior Wildflower Club is a fantastic opportunity for children to explore the park's diverse array of wildflowers. Upon joining, kids receive a wildflower guidebook and a badge to fill with stickers as they spot and identify different flowers throughout their visit. Encourage your child to create a wildflower journal and document their discoveries, deepening their understanding of the park's delicate ecosystem.

Nature Centers and Exhibits: Take your children to the various nature centers and exhibits located within Shenandoah National Park. These educational spaces feature interactive displays, informative exhibits, and knowledgeable staff who can answer questions and provide insights into the park's natural and cultural heritage. Visit the Byrd Visitor Center, Dickey Ridge Visitor Center, or the Harry F. Byrd, Sr. Visitor Center to explore the exhibits and engage in engaging discussions about the park's geology, wildlife, and conservation efforts.

Night Sky Programs: Shenandoah National Park is renowned for its dark skies, presenting a unique opportunity for children to learn about astronomy. Attend a night sky program where rangers and volunteers share their expertise about constellations, planets, and celestial phenomena. Your children will be captivated by the wonders of the universe as they gaze at the starry night sky through telescopes and participate in engaging discussions about our vast universe.

Educational Hikes and Trails: Utilize the park's numerous family-friendly trails as a platform for teaching your children about nature and conservation. Along these trails, you'll find interpretive signs that provide insights into the surrounding ecosystem. Use these informative markers as teaching tools to impart knowledge about the park's plants, animals, and geological features as you hike with your children.

By immersing your children in these educational opportunities, you'll foster their appreciation for the natural world while creating unforgettable family moments.

Chapter 8: Safety Guidelines and Considerations

Weather and Safety Precautions

When exploring the stunning landscapes of Shenandoah National Park, your safety should be a top priority. With its diverse terrain and unpredictable weather, being adequately prepared is essential. By following these safety guidelines, you can ensure a safe and enjoyable trip to Shenandoah National Park:

Checking Weather Conditions: Before embarking on your outdoor adventure, check the weather forecast for the specific area you plan to explore. Shenandoah National Park spans a vast expanse, which means weather conditions can vary greatly. Pay attention to temperature changes, precipitation forecasts, and any severe weather warnings. Remember that higher elevations may experience different weather patterns compared to lower areas.

Dressing Appropriately: Shenandoah National Park's weather can change rapidly, so dressing in layers is crucial. Opt for moisture-wicking and quick-drying fabrics to keep comfortable as you explore. Sturdy footwear is essential for hiking trails, and a waterproof jacket, hat, and gloves will protect you from rain and cooler temperatures.

Carrying Essential Gear: Packing the right gear ensures you'll be prepared for any unexpected situations. Carry a reliable map, compass, or GPS device to navigate the park. Don't forget to pack a whistle, which can be a lifesaver in emergencies. A first aid kit with basic supplies, sunscreen, insect repellent, and any necessary medications should also be included. Additionally, bring enough water and high-energy snacks to keep yourself hydrated and fueled during your adventures.

Being Aware of Lightning Risks: Thunderstorms are common in Shenandoah National Park, especially during the summer months. If you hear thunder, seek shelter immediately in a sturdy building or fully enclosed vehicle. Avoid open areas, tall trees, and exposed ridges, as they attract lightning. If caught in an open area during a storm, crouch down, minimizing your contact with the ground and staying away from nearby objects.

Leave No Trace Principles

Preserving the natural beauty of Shenandoah National Park is crucial for its continued ecological integrity. By following the Leave No Trace principles, you can minimize your impact and help maintain the park's pristine condition:

Thorough Planning: Before your visit, research park regulations, hiking trails, and camping areas. Obtain necessary permits and understand specific rules and recommendations for activities you plan to engage in. This preparation ensures you can minimize your impact and respect the park's delicate ecosystems.

Proper Waste Disposal: Carry a trash bag with you at all times and make sure to pack out all trash, including food waste and wrappers. Dispose of waste in designated receptacles or take it with you to dispose of outside the park. Human waste should be properly disposed of in designated toilets or by digging catholes six to eight inches deep away from water sources, trails, and campsites.

Leave What You Find: Preserve the natural features, historical artifacts, and cultural sites of the park by leaving them untouched. Avoid collecting souvenirs like plants, rocks, or artifacts, as they belong in their natural habitat for future visitors to appreciate.

Minimize Campfire Impacts: If you choose to have a campfire, use designated fire rings or grates when available. Only use dead and downed wood for fuel and keep the fire small to reduce its impact. Ensure the fire is completely extinguished before leaving the campsite. Alternatively, consider using a camp stove for cooking, as it leaves a smaller ecological footprint.

Emergency Contacts

Although Shenandoah National Park is a place of tranquility, it's important to be prepared for emergencies. Familiarize yourself with these contact details for a swift response if needed:

Park Emergency Services: In the event of an emergency within the park, contact Shenandoah National Park Emergency Services at +1 (800) 732-0911. Provide your accurate location, a clear description of the emergency, and any relevant details to help responders assist you promptly.

Local Law Enforcement: Dial 911 in case of emergencies that require immediate police or law enforcement assistance.

Medical Emergencies: If you or someone in your group requires medical assistance, call 911 and provide your location within the park. Accurately describe the nature of the medical situation to ensure an appropriate response.

It's essential to carry a cell phone with dependable reception during your visit to Shenandoah National Park. Keep in mind that cell service can be limited in certain areas, so it's wise to note the locations of emergency phones along Skyline Drive or other established communication points within the park.

By following these safety guidelines, respecting the principles of Leave No Trace, and being aware of emergency contacts, you'll have a safe and memorable experience during your visit to Shenandoah National Park.

Chapter 9: Sample Itineraries

Weekend Itinerary

Day 1: Saturday

Morning

Arrival and Orientation at Thornton Gap Entrance Station

- Time: 8:00 am
- Location: Mile 31.5, Skyline Drive
- Start your weekend adventure by entering the park at the Thornton Gap Entrance Station. Pick up maps and information, and pay your entrance fee.

Hike to Marys Rock

- Time: 8:30 am
- Location: Mile 31.6

This moderate 3.7-mile round-trip hike to Marys Rock offers stunning panoramic views of the Shenandoah Valley and the Blue Ridge Mountains. The trail is well-marked and provides a good mix of forested paths and rocky outcrops.

- Duration: Approximately 2-3 hours

Afternoon

Lunch at Skyland Resort

- Time: 12:00 pm
- Location: Mile 41.7, Skyline Drive

- Enjoy a hearty lunch at Skyland Resort's Pollock Dining Room, which offers spectacular views and a variety of dishes to suit all tastes.

Visit the Byrd Visitor Center

- Time: 1:30 pm
- Location: Mile 51.2, Big Meadows
- The Byrd Visitor Center provides exhibits on the park's history, wildlife, and conservation efforts. It's a great place to learn more about the park's background and significance.

Explore Dark Hollow Falls Trail

- Time: 2:30 pm
- Location: Mile 50.7, Skyline Drive

This short but steep 1.4-mile round-trip hike leads you to one of the park's most beautiful waterfalls. The trail is well-maintained and offers a refreshing walk-through lush forest scenery.

- Duration: Approximately 1-1.5 hours

Evening

Dinner at Big Meadows Lodge

- Time: 5:30 pm
- Location: Mile 51.2, Big Meadows
- After a day of hiking, enjoy a relaxing dinner at Big Meadows Lodge's Spottswood Dining Room. The menu features regional specialties and offers a cozy atmosphere.

Sunset at Blackrock Summit

- Time: 7:30 pm
- Location: Mile 84.4, Skyline Drive
- Trail Details: Blackrock Summit is an easy 1-mile round-trip hike. The rocky outcrop at the summit provides an excellent vantage point for watching the sunset over the Shenandoah Valley.

- Duration: Approximately 1 hour

Stay Overnight at Skyland Resort

- Time: 9:00 pm

- Location: Mile 41.7, Skyline Drive

- End your day by checking in at Skyland Resort. Enjoy the comfort of your room and the peaceful ambiance of the park at night.

Day 2: Sunday

Morning

Breakfast at Skyland Resort

- Time: 7:30 am
- Location: Mile 41.7, Skyline Drive
- Start your day with a delicious breakfast at the resort's dining room, offering a range of options to fuel your morning activities.

Hike the Limberlost Trail

- Time: 8:30 am
- Location: Mile 43, Skyline Drive

This easy 1.3-mile loop is wheelchair accessible and features a beautiful forested area with mountain laurel, large boulders, and a wooden boardwalk.

- Duration: Approximately 1 hour

Afternoon

Lunch at Big Meadows Picnic Grounds

- Time: 12:00 pm
- Location: Mile 51.2, Skyline Drive

- Pack a picnic lunch and enjoy it at the Big Meadows Picnic Grounds. This area offers picnic tables and grills, making it a perfect spot to relax and enjoy the outdoors.

Hike to Lewis Falls

- Time: 1:30 pm
- Location: Mile 51.4, Skyline Drive
- Trail Details: This 3.3-mile round-trip hike takes you to Lewis Falls, an 81-foot waterfall. The trail offers beautiful forest scenery and an impressive view of the falls.
- Duration: Approximately 2-3 hours

Evening

Visit Rapidan Camp

- Time: 4:30 pm
- Location: Mile 51.4, Skyline Drive (requires a 4-mile hike or a scheduled tour)
- Rapidan Camp was President Herbert Hoover's summer retreat. You can visit this historic site either by hiking or joining a ranger-led tour. Explore the buildings and learn about the camp's history and Hoover's time in the park.
- Duration: Approximately 1.5-2 hours

Dinner at a Nearby Town

- Time: 7:00 pm
- Location: Luray, VA
- Head to the nearby town of Luray for dinner. Enjoy a meal at one of the local restaurants, such as the Mimslyn Inn or Gathering Grounds, which offer a variety of dining options.

Return to Your Accommodation or Head Home

- Time: 8:30 pm
- After dinner, return to your accommodation in or near the park, or start your journey home if you prefer. Reflect on a weekend well

spent exploring the natural beauty and historic charm of Shenandoah National Park.

This weekend itinerary provides a balanced mix of hiking, sightseeing, and relaxation, allowing you to fully experience the diverse attractions and activities that Shenandoah National Park has to offer.

1-Day Hiking Itinerary

Morning

Start at the Thornton Gap Entrance Station

Begin your day early by entering the park through the Thornton Gap Entrance Station. This will give you a full day to explore and enjoy the park's offerings.

Old Rag Mountain Hike

- Time: 7:00 am
- Location: Old Rag Mountain, located near the park's eastern boundary.
- Trail Details: This is one of Shenandoah's most popular and challenging hikes, spanning approximately 9.2 miles round-trip. The hike involves rock scrambles, so it's suitable for experienced hikers looking for an adventurous start to their day.
- The summit offers panoramic views of the surrounding mountains and valleys, making the strenuous climb well worth the effort.

Mid-Morning Break

- Time: 10:30 am
- Activity: Take a break at the summit of Old Rag Mountain. Enjoy a snack and hydrate while soaking in the incredible views. This is a great time to rest and take photos.

Afternoon

Lunch at Big Meadows:

- Time: 12:30 pm
- Location: Big Meadows (mile 51.2 on Skyline Drive)
- Activity: Drive to Big Meadows for a relaxing lunch. You can bring a packed lunch to enjoy at one of the picnic areas or dine at the Spottswood Dining Room in Big Meadows Lodge. The lodge offers a variety of dishes, including vegetarian and vegan options.

Dark Hollow Falls Trail:

- Time: 2:00 pm
- Location: Dark Hollow Falls Trail (mile 50.7)
- Trail Details: This 1.4-mile round-trip hike is one of the park's most accessible waterfall hikes. The trail descends steeply to the base of the falls, so be prepared for a bit of a workout on the return ascent.
- Dark Hollow Falls is a beautiful, cascading waterfall. The cool, misty air around the falls provides a refreshing respite after your morning hike.

Skyline Drive Scenic Overlooks:

- Time: 3:30 pm
- Activity: Take a leisurely drive along Skyline Drive, stopping at various scenic overlooks. Key stops include:
- Pinnacles Overlook (mile 36.7): Offers expansive views of the Shenandoah Valley.
- Crescent Rock Overlook (mile 44.4): Great views of Hawksbill Mountain, the highest peak in the park.
- Thornton Hollow Overlook (mile 27.6): A picturesque spot for photographs.

Evening

Hike to Stony Man Summit:

- Time: 5:00 pm
- Location: Stony Man Trail (mile 41.7)

- Trail Details: This 1.6-mile round-trip hike is relatively easy and suitable for all skill levels. The trail leads to the summit of Stony Man Mountain, providing excellent views of the park.
- Highlights: The summit offers panoramic views, making it a perfect spot to relax and reflect on the day's adventures.

Dinner at Skyland:

- Time: 6:30 pm
- Location: Pollock Dining Room, Skyland Resort (mile 41.7)
- Activity: Enjoy a delicious dinner at the Pollock Dining Room. The restaurant serves a variety of meals, often featuring live music for a pleasant dining experience. After a day of hiking and exploration, this is a great way to unwind and enjoy a hearty meal.

Sunset at Little Stony Man Overlook:

- Time: 8:00 pm
- Location: Little Stony Man Overlook (mile 39.1)
- Activity: End your day by watching the sunset from the Little Stony Man Overlook. This spot offers stunning views as the sun sets over the mountains, casting a golden glow over the landscape.

Return to Thornton Gap:

- Time: 9:00 pm
- Activity: Drive back to the Thornton Gap Entrance Station to conclude your day. Reflect on the beautiful sights and experiences you've had in Shenandoah National Park.

This 1-day hiking itinerary ensures you experience some of the best hikes and scenic spots in Shenandoah National Park. By starting early and pacing your activities throughout the day, you can enjoy a fulfilling adventure in this stunning natural setting.

1-Day Skyline Drive Itinerary

Morning

Start at Front Royal Entrance Station:

- Time: 7:00 am
- Location: Front Royal Entrance Station (Mile 0)
- Begin your journey early to take advantage of the entire day. Skyline Drive begins at Front Royal, the northernmost entrance to Shenandoah National Park.

Stop at Dickey Ridge Visitor Center:

- Time: 7:30 am
- Location: Mile 4.6
- Activity: Your first stop is the Dickey Ridge Visitor Center. Pick up maps, talk to rangers for the latest park updates, and explore the exhibits that provide an overview of the park's history and wildlife. Enjoy the view from the nearby overlook before continuing your drive.

Hike the Fox Hollow Trail:

- Time: 8:00 am
- Location: Mile 4.6
- Trail Details: This 1.2-mile loop trail is an easy hike that takes you through a historic farm site. It's a great way to stretch your legs and get a taste of the park's history and natural beauty early in the day.

Skyline Drive Scenic Overlooks:

- Time: 9:00 am
- Location: Various locations along Skyline Drive
- Activity: Continue your drive, stopping at overlooks like Signal Knob (Mile 5.5), Hogback Overlook (Mile 20.8), and Little Stony Man (Mile 39.1). Each offers unique and stunning views of the

Shenandoah Valley and surrounding mountains. Spend time at each overlook, taking photos and appreciating the vistas.

Afternoon

Lunch at Skyland Resort:

- Time: 12:00 pm
- Location: Mile 41.7
- Activity: Stop for lunch at the Skyland Resort, which offers dining options with beautiful views. The Pollock Dining Room serves a variety of meals, including local specialties. Enjoy a leisurely meal and take in the panoramic views from the restaurant.

Hike the Stony Man Trail:

- Time: 1:00 pm
- Location: Mile 41.7
- Trail Details: This 1.6-mile round-trip hike is relatively easy and offers some of the best views in the park. The trail leads to the summit of Stony Man, the second-highest peak in Shenandoah National Park, where you'll be rewarded with breathtaking vistas.

Continue South on Skyline Drive:

- Time: 2:30 pm
- Location: Various locations along Skyline Drive
- Activity: After your hike, continue your drive south. Stop at popular overlooks such as Pinnacles (Mile 36.7) and Crescent Rock (Mile 44.4). Each stop provides different perspectives of the park's diverse landscapes.

Explore Big Meadows:

- Time: 3:30 pm
- Location: Mile 51.2
- Activity: Big Meadows is one of the most famous and accessible spots in Shenandoah National Park. Visit the Big Meadows Lodge, and the Byrd Visitor Center, and walk around the

expansive meadow. This area is known for its wildlife sightings, so keep an eye out for deer and other animals.

Dark Hollow Falls Trail:

- Time: 4:30 pm
- Location: Mile 50.7
- Trail Details: This 1.4-mile round-trip hike is one of the park's most popular. It's a short but steep hike to the base of Dark Hollow Falls, a beautiful cascading waterfall. The trail is well-maintained and offers a refreshing break from driving.

Evening

Dinner at Big Meadows Lodge:

- Time: 6:00 pm
- Location: Mile 51.2
- Activity: After your hike, return to Big Meadows Lodge for dinner. The Spottswood Dining Room offers a cozy atmosphere and a menu featuring regional dishes. Enjoy a relaxing meal and reflect on the day's adventures.

Sunset at Blackrock Summit:

- Time: 7:30 pm
- Location: Mile 84.4
- Trail Details: Blackrock Summit is an easy 1-mile round-trip hike that's perfect for catching the sunset. The trail leads to a rocky outcrop with expansive views of the Shenandoah Valley. Arrive in time to watch the sun dip below the horizon, casting a warm glow over the landscape.

Drive to Rockfish Gap Entrance Station:

- Time: 8:30 pm
- Location: Mile 105

- Activity: Continue your drive south to the Rockfish Gap Entrance Station, the southern end of Skyline Drive. This final leg of your journey allows you to experience the park as the evening sets in.

Return to Starting Point:

- Time: 9:30 pm
- Location: Return to your starting point or head to your accommodation for the night. Reflect on a day well spent exploring the stunning scenery and natural wonders of Shenandoah National Park.

This 1-day itinerary on Skyline Drive allows you to experience the best of what Shenandoah National Park has to offer. From breathtaking overlooks and serene hikes to picturesque waterfalls and abundant wildlife, your journey on Skyline Drive will leave you with unforgettable memories and a deeper appreciation for this beautiful national park.

Conclusion and Recommendations

Congratulations on completing your journey through the Shenandoah National Park Guidebook. As you reflect on the wealth of information and experiences contained within these pages, you've gained invaluable insights into one of America's most cherished natural treasures. From scenic overlooks to historic landmarks, from thrilling outdoor adventures to cultural immersion, Shenandoah National Park offers something for every traveler seeking to explore the wonders of the great outdoors.

Reflecting on Your Experience

Throughout your exploration of Shenandoah National Park, you've had the opportunity to delve into its diverse landscapes, rich history, and vibrant culture. You've ventured along scenic trails, marveled at cascading waterfalls, and witnessed breathtaking vistas from the park's mountaintops. You've immersed yourself in the stories of those who have called this region home, from Native American tribes to early settlers and Civil War soldiers. And you've embraced the sense of wonder and awe that comes from connecting with nature in its purest form.

Recommendations for Future Adventures

As you continue your journey beyond the pages of this guidebook, consider these recommendations for enhancing your Shenandoah experience:

- Exploration Beyond the Beaten Path: While the guidebook highlights many popular attractions and activities, don't hesitate to venture off the beaten path and discover hidden gems within the park. Explore lesser-known trails, seek out secluded overlooks, and immerse yourself in the quiet beauty of Shenandoah's backcountry.
- Embrace the Seasons: Shenandoah National Park transforms with the changing seasons, each offering its unique charms and opportunities for exploration. Whether you're marveling at spring

wildflowers, swimming in mountain streams during the summer, witnessing the fiery hues of fall foliage, or experiencing the tranquility of winter snowfall, each season brings its magic to the park.

- Engage with Park Rangers and Programs: Take advantage of the interpretive programs, ranger-led activities, and educational workshops offered throughout the year. Engage with park rangers, participate in guided hikes, and attend cultural events and festivals to deepen your understanding of Shenandoah's natural and cultural heritage.

- Practice Responsible Stewardship: As you explore Shenandoah National Park, remember to leave no trace and practice responsible outdoor ethics. Respect wildlife and their habitats, stay on designated trails and leave the park as you found it to ensure that future generations can continue to enjoy its beauty for years to come.

Benefits of Using This Guidebook

By utilizing the Shenandoah National Park Guidebook, you've gained access to comprehensive information, insider tips, and expert recommendations to help you make the most of your visit. From planning your itinerary to navigating the park's trails and discovering its hidden treasures, this guidebook has been your trusted companion every step of the way.

Through detailed descriptions, helpful maps, and engaging narratives, the guidebook has provided you with the tools and resources needed to create unforgettable memories and meaningful experiences in Shenandoah National Park. Whether you're a first-time visitor or a seasoned explorer, this guidebook has empowered you to embark on a journey of discovery, adventure, and connection to the natural world.

As you bid farewell to Shenandoah National Park, may the memories you've created and the experiences you've shared be a source of inspiration for future adventures. From the towering peaks of the Blue

Ridge Mountains to the serene valleys and meandering streams below, Shenandoah's beauty will continue to beckon, inviting you to return time and time.

Thank you for allowing the Shenandoah National Park Guidebook to be your companion on this extraordinary journey. May your adventures in Shenandoah and beyond be filled with wonder, discovery, and the boundless joys of exploration until we meet again, happy trails and safe travels!

Shenandoah National Park Travel Planner

Shenandoah National Park

Travel Planner 2024

Date:_____

Town:_____

Monday	Tuesday	Wednesday

Thursday	Friday	Saturday

Checklist	Note

Shenandoah National Park

Travel Planner 2024

Date:_____

Town:_____

Monday	Tuesday	Wednesday

Thursday	Friday	Saturday

Checklist	Note

Shenandoah National Park

Travel Planner 2024

Date:_____

Town:_____

Monday	Tuesday	Wednesday

Thursday	Friday	Saturday

Checklist	Note

Shenandoah National Park
Travel Planner 2024

Date:_____

Town:_____

Monday	Tuesday	Wednesday

Thursday	Friday	Saturday

Checklist	Note

146

Shenandoah National Park

Date:_____

Town:_____

Travel Planner 2024

Monday	Tuesday	Wednesday

Thursday	Friday	Saturday

Checklist	Note

Shenandoah National Park

Date:_____

Town:_____

Travel Planner 2024

Monday	Tuesday	Wednesday

Thursday	Friday	Saturday

Checklist	Note

Shenandoah National Park Travel Itinerary

Name:	Duration of Stay:

Hotel Name:	
Arrival Date:	Flight No:

Days	What To Do	Budget
01		
02		
03		
04		
Note		

Name:		Duration of Stay:
Hotel Name:		Flight No:
Arrival Date:		

Days	What To Do	Budget
01		
02		
03		
04		
Note		

Name:		Duration of Stay:
Hotel Name:		
Arrival Date:		Flight No:

Days	What To Do	Budget
01		
02		
03		
04		
Note		

Name:		**Duration of Stay:**
Hotel Name:		**Flight No:**
Arrival Date:		

Days	What To Do	Budget
01		
02		
03		
04		
Note		

Name:		Duration of Stay:
Hotel Name:		Flight No:
Arrival Date:		

Days	What To Do	Budget
01		
02		
03		
04		
Note		

Made in the USA
Middletown, DE
16 September 2024

61016815R00091